Coming Through Fire

Coming Through Fire

The Wildland Firefighter Experience

Text by David Greer
Photography by Noel Hendrickson

RAINCOAST BOOKS

Vancouver

First published in 2001 by

Raincoast Books
9050 Shaughnessy Street
Vancouver, B.C.
V6P 6E5
(604) 323-7100

www.raincoast.com

1 2 3 4 5 6 7 8 9 10

CANADIAN CATALOGUING IN PUBLICATION DATA

Hendrickson, Noel, 1970–
Coming through fire

ISBN 1-55192-324-6

1. Wildfires—British Columbia. 2. Wildfires—British Columbia—Pictorial works. 3. Wildfire fighters—British Columbia.
I. Greer, David, 1968– II. Title.

SD421.34.C3H46 2000   634.9'618'09711   C00-910526-3

Designed by Susan MacPherson

Printed in Hong Kong, China

Raise your glass to the men and women of fire. You are a rare bunch and although you have left us permanently warped, we are indebted to you. Thank you for inspiring in us a renewed sense of humour, and for giving us strength of character, integrity, and solemn deter-mination, all of which have been at the heart of our many lasting friendships ... Cheers!

CONTENTS

"On forest fires there are moments almost solely for beauty. Such moments are of short duration."
— Norman MacLean

FOREWORD

by Jim Dunlop, former director, British Columbia Forest Service Protection Branch

In the old days the British Columbia Forest Service would recruit firefighters from wherever they could be found. In the 1950s and 1960s a lot of firefighters were from the logging industry. We would go into logging camps to call in buckers, fallers and all these guys who knew how to work in the bush. Recruits got no traditional training in those days, and no safety equipment aside from hardhats. In some cases a pump and hose would be dropped off at a fire, where supervisors would simply say, "Start it up and put the fire out." It is probably the best training there is — with flames licking your butt. I say it wasn't Nike that came up with the phrase "Just Do It," it was the Forest Service in 1958.

It wasn't until the late 1980s that we started to professionalize the firefighting ranks. Now everyone on the fireline is a *professional* firefighter. They are trained, experienced and physically fit. At one time it was not uncommon to have more than 10,000 people go through the payroll system in a summer. Now we have 1,000 firefighters who do the whole job, and half of their time is spent out of province. These days the production level is so much higher.

Whether we're speaking of today or 40 years ago, firefighting is a very demanding business. But it's also a business that creates a strong bond among its participants. As a wildland firefighter, you feel obligated to make yourself available to fires. I once took a holiday in Mexico for two weeks and spent it sitting on the bed with the phone in my ear, talking to guys about fire. If you are going to be a firefighter, and you are going to stay in it forever, you might as well kiss your summers goodbye. But it's an exciting job — and the rewards are many.

Each year thousands of forest fires threaten wildlife habitats, natural resources and public safety around the world. And each year thousands of brave and dedicated women and men go to battle to protect society and the things it holds valuable. In British Columbia, some of the world's best firefighters literally put their lives on the line to protect their province's forests and homes. These firefighters — whose work lives are documented in this book — are a close-knit group who care about their jobs, their province and each other.

INTRODUCTION

by David Greer

Every year, beginning early in May, I leave behind my home and occasionally a lover and take to the wildlands of British Columbia and other provinces to work for the summer. My life has become seasonal, revolving around the summer months when I am employed in the best job in the world, a job that challenges me physically, mentally and emotionally.

When my friend and fellow wildland firefighter Noel Hendrickson first told me in 1998 about his desire to create a book on forest firefighting, he asked me to search my journals and find words to accompany his photographs. In its infancy, this project involved many evenings viewing slides, talking about our fireline days, drinking cocktails and having an inspirational Skoal or two. Overall, Noel wanted me to provide some explanation for his pictures, and to convey the experience of our intense summers. When I pulled five years' worth of journals out of my storage boxes, I remembered just how intense those summers were. The emotion of my writing surprised me. Reading the entries, I also realized the influence that my firefighting career has had on my life. In some cases, I found that much of my writing was too personal to reveal to anyone.

When I visit Noel, I always take out his numerous photo albums that span our firefighting careers — from our year as rookies up to the present — and I am always surprised and overwhelmed by how I feel. My memory is awakened and I either laugh out loud or become contemplative when I remember some of the hardest, dirtiest and happiest days of my life. I can't believe how dirty we get — it's always such a contrast to the state of cleanliness and comfort in which we view the photographs. I miss my friends when I see their faces. These people, my crewmates, are dynamic in many ways, and they have to be. We all live in such close quarters. We eat breakfast, lunch and dinner together, we work all day together, and then we play together. At night we share tents and stories with each other. We grow to love and hate each other. We develop valuable physical, mental and social skills together. After the fire season, these experiences and skills stay with me for the rest of the year.

In the past six fire seasons, Noel has been obsessive about taking his camera everywhere. I chide him for his constant fussing every morning as he prepares his equipment for the day. He carries a heavier bag than the rest of us as we hike and work in and around the fire. Every night he unpacks, cleans and maintains his gear. Noel's gear has become such an intimate part of him that we hardly notice it anymore. We have become unconscious of his camera and his craft. Noel repeats his rituals every day whether or not photos are to be taken on that day — I struggle to remember my pen and notebook.

As a firefighter for the British Columbia Forest Service I am proud to be part of the long history of forest fire prevention and suppression. Forest firefighters have worked to protect our homes, our land and our valuable timber resources from the destructive force of fire since 1905, when four wardens were appointed to help prevent forest fires. My father fought fire in British Columbia in the 1960s, and he still enjoys telling his many stories, especially those that involve encounters with the Martin Mars water bomber. We compare stories of seeing the majestic Mars flying just above the treetops and dropping its enormous payload on the raging fire below. We compare firefighting technology and techniques, and it becomes clear that great progress in forest firefighting tools, theory and safety has been made over the years. The latest technologies are now employed to track lightning and to locate fires; teams of skilled personnel analyze fire activity and resources to coordinate plans of attack. As a member of a 20-person ground crew, I appreciate the technology that is employed to aid us in fighting fire; yet I am most proud to be part of a tradition that involves pulaskis, shovels, dirt and hard physical work. In a society in which more and more people are employed in high-technology jobs that involve desks and computers, I am fortunate to be privy to the awesome forces of nature, and to be able to work the earth for long hours, days on end.

Coming Through Fire is the collaborative work of two forest firefighters working in different mediums — photography and writing. Noel and I wanted to combine our skills to create a book that would recreate the firefighting experience for our readers. With this in mind, we organized the book in a way that would take the reader from the beginning of the fire season through to its end. Along the way, we explain how we work a fire — be sure to refer to the glossary at the back of the book, which provides definitions for terminology you may find unfamiliar. We also present a "case study" of a specific fire — the 1998 fire at Salmon Arm. One of the worst forest fires ever to occur in the province of British Columbia, it damaged more than 6,000 hectares, destroyed 40 buildings and led to the evacuation of nearly 7,000 people. The voices of other firefighters are presented throughout the book. Noel has contributed some of his own writing, as have our peers — after all, it is *their* book. In *Coming Through Fire*, we have endeavoured to present to our audience the most authentic record of the wildland firefighter experience.

"Grubbing an ashpit with water support is one thing, dry-mopping is quite another. Steaming hot ash and silt flood our boots and hard-bake our pants. Usually we'll work in pairs, tagging off and holding our breath for as long as we can while we mix it up."
— *Noel Hendrickson*

THE HUMAN ELEMENT

by David Greer

Fire has fascinated and mesmerized humans from the time of its discovery. Many myths tell of the discovery of fire, but it is most likely that humans first encountered fire after a lightning strike and subsequent forest fire. In his intriguing book, *Myths of the Origin of Fire*, Sir James George Frazer writes about ancient tribes who generated myths about how they discovered fire and the spiritual significance it had for their people. Frazer writes of the inhabitants of Mangaia in the Cook Islands who say that their ancestors obtained fire from a great conflagration and used it to cook their food but, when it went out, they had no idea how to rekindle it. "Even when men have long been in possession of fire," Frazer writes, "they are apt to regard with peculiar awe and veneration a fire which has been kindled by a flash of lightning, thus the Oraons of Chota Nagpur in India, though they do not originally consider fire as sacred, esteem 'lightning fire' as 'sent by heaven.'"[1]

Lightning accounts for about 40 percent of all forest fires in British Columbia. When thunder and lightning storms crash near our camp in the Kootenays, I become restless and notice my crewmates restlessly beginning their rituals. I like to stand at the fence that borders our camp, watch for lightning and let the rain soak me when it comes. When the lightning show is particularly impressive, I band with everyone standing at the fence and we get into a vehicle and chase the lightning up the valley. We pull over at the appropriate times to watch lightning dart behind mountains and crash around corners. Some of my crewmates go down to the dock by the river and howl as the rain escalates until you begin to wonder if it could possibly rain any harder — then it does, soaking you so much that you feel compelled to dive into the river.

Other crewmates pace around camp — from the laundry trailer to the kitchen, to the office, to the warehouse, thinking they have some odd job there, then move on to their tent or to the television tent, where others are absorbed in a movie. Some crewmates simply sit in their tent and read, while others lay in their cots and ruminate uneasily. A flash of lightning always arouses us, and dry lightning is even more exciting. Then I know I'll find my crewmates at the fence watching for potential starts in the mountains, flaring orange against the sky.

As forest firefighters, we have the privilege of being able to work with and experience the natural phenomenon of fire. We are awed and inspired by fire no matter how often we encounter it. We both love and hate it — we fear it and fight against it, yet we respect it and are awed by it. Fire feeds off the land, and we feed off the energy of the fire.

When we first approach a forest fire, we quickly become aware of its behaviour and its power. The fire dictates the energy the crew generates in order to control and contain it. A large fire that spreads rapidly heightens everyone's physical and mental alertness; group dynamics and excitement reach great heights and everyone becomes anxious to work. But the latter days of a fire dampen energy levels as the fire gives up and hides from us. It hides in the form of invisible hotspots that usually can be detected only by smell. At this stage we are fatigued, yet we search to hit them all. As the fire becomes controlled and the immediate danger is diminished, we separate from each other as we spread out to reach more scarce and scattered hotspots.

We patrol and search the same territory day after day — endlessly walking and sniffing out hotspots on a stark grey and black landscape. Daily life becomes monotonous as we see the same faces every morning when we wake up, and continue to see them throughout the day: at breakfast, work, lunch, dinner, after dinner and before we go to bed. Even at night they sometimes show up in dreams or nightmares. Fatigue sets in on the body but also on the mind, as there is less and less excitement to look forward to. The fire is waning and so is our energy.

Firefighters who are funny, witty and entertaining make valuable company during the latter days of a fire. They can make you laugh or make you think about something other than what you have been dwelling on for the last hundred hours or so. It's not unusual for a sustained attack crew to work 13- to 15-hour days for 14 days straight, take two days off, and then travel to a new fire where the anticipation and excitement starts all over again. Long hours worked for several days in a row enable firefighters to think about their past, present, and future lives several thousand times over. The best firefighters have the mental ability and the physical conditioning to work long hours for several days in a row and still maintain their acuity, which is crucial, as mental sharpness results in fewer bad, unsafe decisions.

Firefighters come from a variety of backgrounds. One trait that most, if not all firefighters have in common is physical vigour. We engage in physical activity year round and usually have an affinity for the outdoors. The majority of firefighters are also competitive and team-oriented — qualities essential for fighting fire. It takes a huge mass of spirit and energy to confront a fire's mass of spirit and energy. Competitiveness is evident when we play sports together as a crew. It becomes clear that no one likes to lose, and this is a good attitude to take to the fireline.

We are constantly trying to improve our skills, so we become better at our work, and therefore more valuable to the crew. Every crew is an assembly of people with diverse talents and assets; an essential combination when faced with myriad situations. We come to appreciate our fellow crew members and their personal contributions and skills. With some crewmates you can trust your

"My first forest fire had somehow altered my outlook on most aspects of existence. On a fire, life consists of sleeping, working and eating. Everything else is secondary. It was four days before any of us could properly wash. Fourteen hours a day of sweat, smoke, dirt and grime add up quickly. The food is a monotony of white bread and mystery meats. By day 10, you could care less about the lack of dietary variety. Yet, despite all this, there is something so damn satisfying about feeling what it's like to work hard and survive. It's incredibly liberating to alter your life, to reduce it such an extreme degree, and to feel more fulfilled and satisfied than ever before." — *Christy Brookes*

deepest troubles and worries; other crewmates are special because they are quiet and peaceful to be around. Some crewmates are intense and excel under pressure. Others are skilled at the art of motivation and have the ability to bring out the best in those around them.

Even when work is finished for the day I'm always assured that friends will be sitting around the campfire after dinner, telling stories and cracking jokes. Fire is always nearby: we all share it in common. I enjoy staring into the fire and getting lost in the flames. I love to spray water into a hotspot and watch it hiss, pop and explode — the hide-and-seek game of the workday continuing into night. Every morning and afternoon at our base we meet at the fire pit and discuss our day plan, and in the evenings we stoke up the fire in our sauna and relax in the dry heat, watching the flicker of flames cast our shadows on the pine walls. The human element is as passionate as the fire itself. Firefighters need to be challenged, fed and inspired by fire, not unlike the ancient tribes of time past.

[1] Sir James George Frazer, *Myths of the Origin of Fire* (London: Macmillan, 1930) 204.

"So here's a song to dirt and sweat,
  A grace to grit and grime;
  A hail to workers who beget
    The wonders of our time.
And as they gaze, through gutter-girt,
    To palaces enskied,
  Let them believe, by sweat and dirt,
    They, too, are glorified."
      — Robert Service

< "The orange of this nighttime fire is so mesmerizing. The sparks appear like fireflies and sparklers." — *David Greer*

> "I've come to appreciate the gift of warmth and the smouldering welcome the fire offers on these icy mornings. Today, we made cappuccinos and toasted our sammies one last time at lunch before we put the fire out." — *Noel Hendrickson*

"I remember this day very clearly. We had been hiking some steep, slide-slope scree all day and we found a spot with an amazing view to stop for lunch and rest our taxed ankles. Everyone was in a contemplative mood since this particular fire had been long and mentally exhausting. We all just lay back and meditated, letting our minds drift deep into the valley. As I look at this photo, it is only in retrospect that I notice the flower in Jeff's right ear. Jeff has always had a calming effect on our crew — at the time I was in my own world."
— *David Greer*

< "One thing I notice at fire camps is that everybody comes to our campfire. There's a good warm family feel as most of us have been working together for more than seven years." — *Ryan Pascal*

> "We rely on one another out here. The combined talent of the individuals who make up this crew is astounding. Sometimes I step back and marvel at the calibre of these people — their skill, ability and determination — and I know it has helped me to grow." — *Chris Gourley*

CAMP LIFE AND CONDITIONING

CAMP LIFE: THE ROOKIE
by Noel Hendrickson

All summers begin the same, with the 20 of us reacquainting ourselves and testing the limits of our wintered bodies. The green ones — "those damn rookies" — are excited about nearly everything. As a veteran, it's your job to appear unenthusiastic, outwardly complacent and unmoved. It's all too easy to forget how you became this thick-skinned lifer, and the pain you suffered as an FNG (see glossary). If I reflect back on the lessons learned, specifically the humiliation I went through, I can clearly visualize my first day in camp.

"So, yer sure you wanna get off in South Slocan?" My watch reads 3:00 a.m, and I think: *South? North? What's the difference? It's a small town.* I tell my driver, "South Slocan will be perfect." Loaded down with four of the heaviest bags I've ever packed — and I'm known for my excessive baggage — I shuffle down the still-dark highway to a green sign which makes the bus driver's question ring loudly in my head: *South Slocan 1 km, Slocan City 48 km.* I crumple over my mountain of bags and wait in the drizzle for two-and-a-half hours before a logger picks me up on his way to work. *Slocan at last.* I decide that I should ask for directions and grab a coffee at the local café. As the waitress pours, she seems to be sizing me up — "Firefighters, eh? You guys starting up early this year? Still run at 10:30 on Tuesdays and Thursdays?" "I guess," I answer. I later discover that some of the women in town watch us during physical training on Tuesdays and Thursdays, gathering along our running route to ogle shirtless firefighters.

With the waitress's directions I balance my cargo and scuttle into the beautiful fire camp nestled in the cedar forest next to the town dump. Two guys, both in their underwear, are carrying a bed from the dump into camp. One is dark and hairy, and the other pale and pudgy with huge quads. "Hey, new guy, what's your name?" the pale one says. "I'm Noel." "Oh you're Stace's friend. I'm Mike and this is Craig. Gimme a second and I'll show you around." Mike, the pale one, gives me the tour, then leaves me to settle in. "Hey Mike, what tent should I stay in?" I ask. "Well since you're a rookie, you'd be in the rookie tent. Rookie." Inside are the four other guys with whom I've survived a rigorous boot camp. It feels good to see some friendly faces. Feeling more confident and even more annoyed at being called a rookie at the age of 23, I go in search of other accommodations. I know one of the 20 scruffy men milling about, half asleep. "Stace, you got any room in your tent?" I ask. He tells me politely that all the spaces have been taken and that I should try The Swamp.

"There is *always* room in The Swamp, rookie," Mike shouts out from under his sleeping bag.

The sloppiest, smelliest, most obstinate vets live in The Swamp. They are proud of the smell and the mess and, already on day one, underwear leaks out the side of the tent, and a single, mangled deer antler hangs in the entrance. I poke my head into the tent — there are clothes everywhere, posters, mattresses, a motorbike in the middle, and three huge scruffy beasts inside. "Hi guys, do you have any ..." "Who the hell are you? Get the fuck out of here, rookie!!" Tail between my legs, I rejoin my rookie brothers and one other, an outcast. In seeking the shelter of our tent, this RFL makes our cramped living conditions even worse. I soon learn that as a new guy, I have no say. I'm at the bottom, expected to prove myself and, until such time, I'm basically ignored.

I never thought I would be that timid again after surviving the "old school" boot camp a week earlier. That week of being treated like scum, of taxing my body to near shutdown, revealed a part of me that I didn't realize I had. Our will to be individuals was nearly broken by militant training tactics, like those used in army boot camps. Those first days united us, cementing rookie friendships that still remain today and are echoed in the reunion cry, *Class of '94*. This cry, the bane of all those who follow, attests to the blood, sweat, tears and vomit endured in the last of the "real" training camps the Forest Service provided. These fabled stories, which we "old school" types seem to perpetuate, have been replaced by recent accounts of a new and softer approach to training recruits where everyone has fun and physical training seems to be semi-optional. No deprivation? No humiliation? No punishments? What can become of this?

Our rookies get a second week of training once they arrive at camp. They are pushed hard and kept separate from the vets; we want them to work as a team, to trust and look out for one another. We take them into the mountains around camp, outfitted in their banana suits, and put them to task. Guard digging, laying hose and hauling impossible amounts of heavy gear up steep inclines, through creeks and down even steeper slopes. They almost never disappoint us, but we always look disappointed — damn rookies. Push-up punishments are the norm when mistakes are made or when the FNGs are too slow — they're always too slow. At the end of the week, the rookies are welcomed to the crew and given their official uniform of reds and blues. Traditionally, Friday night is reserved for a crew get-together at Sam's Pub, where willing rookies are further indoctrinated by drinking "a yard of beer" while the vets relive the glory days.

"If ranger tents could talk, they'd tell one another about crowded floors, leaky corners and stinky boots. They'd speak of roomies who keep them awake at night with godawful snoring and incessant whining. They would compare homemade furniture, dampened bedding, peeling floors and dirty dishes. Complaining of broken zippers, pollen-stained roofs and the lingering scent of skunk, the tents would remain grateful, though, for they have a soft spot for the scruffy smell factories who live inside their walls." — *Noel Hendrickson*

CAMP LIFE: THE VET

by David Greer

Fire camp life consists of two situations: base camp and fireline camp. Base camp is my home for the summer. Here, we don't have Bill Murray for a camp counselor, although parents do visit from time to time. We don't run sack races, just some very competitive foot races. Every physical activity ensures a high level of competition, and those who do well are sure to excel on the fireline, where physical endurance limits are so often taxed. Our required fitness test is our Olympics. Here personal bests are encouraged and applauded. The shuttle run, which has now been replaced by the pack test, and the upright row tests burn out the legs, lungs and upper body, and prepare us for the pump hose test, which involves running several hundred metres while carrying a pump and some heavy hose, then running with a charged fire hose that gets heavier the farther you pull it. My legs recoil in horror and tingle with nervous energy before I start this sprint — they feel like fire when I finish. I think about this test every time I hike up a steep slope with hose slung over my shoulders.

Pranks are also an integral part of camp training. Rookies are the subject of pranks throughout their first year, as are unsuspecting veterans. One of our favourite pranks is called the "chainsaw massacre." While the innocent rookies sleep soundly in their tent, a few nocturnal vets spring into action, bring chainsaws from the warehouse. A short while later the rookies are rudely awakened by the sound of large Husqvarnas revving and flashing beside their cots. Turning on their lights, the rookies see masked marauders advancing toward them with screeching saws. The rookies scream and recoil in horror as the marauders lower the bars upon their retreating legs. Howling in pain, the rookies notice that it's a prank — the chain has been removed from the bar. While their victims soil their sleeping bags, the laughing marauders dash from the tent in a wake of two-stroke smoke and bar oil.

As well as being the site for these various forms of "conditioning," base camp is our meeting place and fire headquarters. The fire pit and the kitchen are where we gather. We meet at the fire pit every morning in our shorts for physical training and daily fire updates. We also meet over chow — two, three or six times a day depending on your size and requirements. Food is the most important aspect of both base and fire camps. The cooks play a pivotal role in our happiness — if we make them unhappy, they will let us know with a few select dishes such as pork wallets. *Pork wallets*, you ask? Well take out your wallet and try to take a bite out of it. Luckily, I'm a vegetarian — or unluckily, since I face a constant barrage of PB&J sandwiches during the summer. The assault is so punitive and unrelenting that I can honestly say that I have never eaten one outside of this job in six years. Fireline meals always consist of bartering, bribing and brisk swapping transactions of

"I have been racing bicycles for the last 10 years — the last four as a pro. I had learned to suffer and ride through pain and fatigue on my bike, so I thought that fitness for Unit Crew was not going to be problem. Upon my arrival at base camp, I quickly learned that I was going to have to cope with new physical challenges. As one of the smaller guys on the crew at 160 pounds, I have to keep up to the big 200-pound boys. I came into camp a bit cocky about my fitness level. However, I quickly learned that it is one thing to ride a mountain bike faster than most people but another thing to lift 10-foot sections of tree onto your shoulder or to carry 100 pounds of equipment up a long 45-degree slope. What a mental challenge to go from being one of the best at what you do, to being average. I have suffered over the last three months trying to keep up with these people physically. Trying to deal with not being the best at what I am doing is not something I am used to."
— *Mike Jones*

foodstuffs. A chocolate bar goes a long way on day 11 of a fire.

Fire camps are also a place to meet firefighters from other crews and faculties — Unit Crew, Parattack, Rapattack, and Initial Attack. Whatever crew we're on, though, we share a common bond: staying healthy, happy and well nourished.

"It is 37°C out here today and we have just finished running 10 kilometres. I think our cook, Alastair, must be mad at us today, because he is torturing us with thick greasy pork smokies for lunch while we sweat in this queasy heat. When he's upset he assaults us with cheeses and tries to kill us with hidden fats in the baking. If we keep out of his hair it's barbequed salmon and wild rice, but if someone pisses him off ..."
— *David Greer*

THE DYSFUNCTIONAL FAMILY

by Noel Hendrickson

"Team" is definitely the wrong word to describe the bizarre cast of characters that I have worked with over the past six summers. Yes, we function as a highly productive team, but it's more like a family. Like so many families, ours is dysfunctional. My 19 brothers and sisters annoy me to no end. And each is as individual as the next — strong in character, loose with opinions and sharp of tongue. Sarcasm and mockery are the daily staples we feed on. The FNG's learn to hone their wit very quickly since we old school types can smell raw meat from miles around.

Abnormality is the norm — it just seems to fit out here. At any one time people are filling your sleeping bag with shaving cream, or hiding dead squirrels in your locker; someone (I won't name names) is wearing your underwear and socks because his are dirty. A weird little fella is staying up late trying to catch the skunk that keeps spraying everyone. Another is down sleeping with the geese on the dock. The group swimming naked down at the river howls at the moon, and another group bickers about which movies to watch. Those damn rookies and RFL's are always on the phone or blocking up the Internet. We have a twisted camp chef who is neither a mother nor father figure, yet treats us like gold and listens to our gossip and inane complaints; we'll miss him when he moves on. It's not unusual to wake up and hear someone screaming at the ravens and squirrels that started squawking and dropping pinecones on the roof at 5:00 a.m. It's just one of those rare environments that nurtures the oft-hidden wild side we all have. We look out for one another in this family and learn to embrace these weird antics as a refreshing reminder that it is simply more fun than repressing them.

< "My lungs are aching and my legs feel like dead weight, but the cheers and support from the rest of the crew help me push through the pain. I take my last few steps toward the finish of the pump-hose test and collapse on the ground fully spent. The fitness test is never about simply passing, it is about competing with peers, pushing personal limits, and is all about a deep sense of pride." — *Jason Crabb*

> "Our fitness standards are set for a reason; anything less would undermine the integrity of the protection program, and it would also undermine the abilities and efforts of firefighters on the fireline. When the fires run, they roar. I am not interested in becoming a casualty, nor am I interested in having to worry that the person next to me will not be able to make it out alive should we ever have to run for it." — *Urve Voitk*

< "We pair up and camp in tents together, establishing micro relationships. The quiet words at night spoken about each other — our crewmates. Oh, the heated arguments, they seem so petty in the fall. Yet out here, now, in this close, tight situation, where every crewmember deserves and insists on equality, things are tense." — *David Greer*

> "Rappelling the waterfall near Camp Valhalla. Chief and The Ginch would disappear beneath the rushing water, then spring out off the rock, hooting and hollering, then plunge back in." — *Noel Hendrickson*

"When I train alone in the off-season, I rarely push myself to the levels of discomfort I reach when I'm training with the crew. Rarely a group of people pushes me to run faster and into a state of stomach-churning, lung-burning madness. We run lined up in pairs, where we are encouraged to keep pace with the people in front, and those breathing heavily behind us."
— *David Greer*

< "There was some downtime at the camp, so I decided to oil up my dry boots and make them handsome again. This job is religious for me. My boot oil is like incense to my nose and its application is as careful, dedicated and crucial as a Japanese tea ceremony." — *David Greer*

> "Sometimes being a woman at fire camp has its advantages, such as experiencing no lineups for showers. My last fire camp had four showers for the men and four showers for the women, only there were 150 of them and seven of us. It was a strange feeling walking past the endless, black and blank faces in the men's lineup on my way into the empty women's washroom." — *Geraldine Woods*

"We step off of the bus, groggy and stunned when we arrive at Camp Happy, Swan Hills, Alberta after a long and bumpy school bus ride. We're told more crews will arrive later, and we're going to have to erect 74 canvas pioneer tents to accommodate everyone. Every tent requires 9 poles. With pulaskis as the only available chopping tools, we hack at a stand of small, hard, burnt timber until we have 666 poles. It starts to drizzle while we are chopping — it really turns ugly when the downpour starts. The ground turns into thick black mud. We start to erect the tents while I dream of a hot dinner. Dinner turns out to be a one-kilometre, balls-deep walk up a muddy road. We sleep in the mud tents of the beautiful Camp Happy Resort for two weeks."
— *David Greer*

"From hotels to trailers to canvas tents, we take what we're given and make the best of it. These pioneer tents are appropriately named, because when they are set up I can hardly resist the urge to eat beans out of a can over an open fire, sleep on the cold hard ground."
— *Noel Hendrickson*

< "The many crews based at the camp mix well, new friendships are formed, and the vets swap old stories. Days pass and the stories grow into epics as old fires become enormous battles in which firefighters performed seemingly inhuman feats of physical labour to put them out." — *Jason Crabb*

> "I don't shave or shower until the end of the last day of the fire. I usually change my sweat-caked pants a couple of times in a two-week duration, but rarely my shirt. When our last day is finished, I enjoy the most heavenly shower and shave possible. My body is absolutely black with thick soot and is so thankful for a hot shower that my pores open up and sing show tunes. This approach to living enables me to never take such things for granted. I still probably enjoy a shave and hot shower more than anyone, except those who also belong to my sick, filthy club." — *David Greer*

FIRELINE

ON THE FIRELINE

by David Greer

People are often intrigued when they find out that I am a forest firefighter and they always ask: "How do you fight a forest fire, don't you dig a ditch or something?" My explanation always includes: "It all depends on the size and wrath of the fire." Keep this phrase in mind and tack it on to the end of every one of the following sentences.

For now, imagine a forest fire of any size, or better yet, a large project fire, which is burning rank one to rank three (see glossary). Usually, we start by cutting a fuel-free — we cut a road around the fire using bodies and chainsaws to clear the trees and brush. This way the fire will run out of fuel once it burns up to the edge of the fuel-free. Quite often while we're creating this fuel-free, helicopters and fixed-wing aircraft drop water on areas that are heating up and have the potential to compromise our work. If the fire's behaviour is too intense and the fire is moving quickly, the fuel-free becomes merely an obstacle that only serves to slow the fire down, not stop it. We hate it when our fuel-frees are breached because it means that we have to do all that work over again. If you yourself sawed or swamped for 12 hours or so, with the scorching heat, the acrid smoke, a crappy lunch and other adverse conditions, you'd know how we feel.

The fuel-free can effectively control or contain the surface fire, but it is less effective at stopping a creeping, lurking, angry, pernicious, dogged and determined ground or subsurface fire. Buckets dropped from a helicopter can slow a fire that is flaring up in the treetops, but the water from the buckets rarely reaches the ground to thwart the tenacious, sneaking and stubborn ground fire. Ground fires burn hot in the duff and moss of the forest floor and climb pre-heated trees that can explode into flames and eventually candle. When several trees start to candle, they tend to ignite the dry tops of other trees. In a wind, the trees will crown and create a huge conflagration that develops its own wind and subsequent firestorm.

To stop this elevated activity, we thwart the lowly ground fire by digging a fireguard in the middle of our fuel-free. This ditch or trench is dug by hand (hand guard) or by bulldozer (Cat guard), if the terrain and conditions permit. The bulldozer also cuts a fuel-break when it smashes through trees with its tall, wide and heavy blade. Firefighters dig hand guards in terrain that is too steep for a Cat, or if Cats are not available because of remoteness, supply or cost. Guards have to be dug down through the duff to mineral soil. No organic material can be left for the fire to burn. The trench has to have clean edges with no roots hanging over it.

The majority of firefighters take great pride in their guards. Hand guards are seen as a true reflection of self and are taken very seriously. Everybody has his or her own style. I dig my guard wider than it has to be and I like to work on long sections regardless of the obstacles, which can include: swamp, big trees (which mean big nasty roots), and fuck brush. When choosing my section, I make sure it's long enough for me to stay there for awhile. I do this because I love to finish my section, then leapfrog the entire crew and check out their work on my way to the front of the line. I like to see how much progress we've made, and I like to critique, cajole and encourage my crewmates on the way. Noel likes to garden in his section. His guard is exceptionally neat. He digs swift, short and sharp sections, then he moves on.

When we have a control line established, we usually lay hose around and direct attack the fire. If no natural water source is accessible, we have to fight the fire with hand tools — by throwing soil on the flames and digging up hotspots — or we have a helicopter drop water into a pumpkin that we can pump out. Sometimes we use skidders that have water tanks and pumps on board. Skidders are useful because they manoeuvre well in unforgiving terrain. I'll try at all costs to find a pump site from which I can obtain a constant supply of clean water — even if I have to dam a creek to get it. Fighting fire without water, or with a poor supply, is time consuming, labour intensive and inefficient, yet it is often quite necessary.

When a fire gets large and its behaviour is aggressive, we "fight fire with fire." As the cliché implies, we light a fire from the control line or starting point, such as a natural fuel-break or fuel-free. This indirect attack is used as a last resort and only if the conditions are favourable. The wind has to be blowing in the right direction — toward the main burn. The back fire consumes the fuel between the control line and the main burn, which then creates a convection and burns the main fire out. It's incredible to watch. We light the back fire manually with drip torches, flame throwers or with helicopters that drop gel balls filled with fuel that are detonated as they leave the helicopter and explode into flame when they hit the ground.

When the situation permits we employ a parallel attack stratagem: we burn off pockets of fuel inside the control line and the main burn in order to starve the fire of fuel. I keep an eye on weather conditions throughout the day. I read the weather in order to predict fire behaviour; essential for safety and fire attack strategy. With weather and fire behaviour, it's best to predict the unpredictable. For a forest firefighter, safety is of the greatest concern. There are thousands of ways and opportunities to be killed, injured or maimed out there, so you always have to CYA.

Spot-fires involve the same strategies as larger fires, without the back fires and burning off. Usually initial Attack squads comprised of three people, including a crew leader, attend spot-fires. More than one squad will combine if the fire is larger. As their job is to stop a fire in its initial

"Most firefighters take great pride in their guards. Hand guards are seen as a true reflection of self and are taken very seriously. — *David Greer*

stages, they attend a lot of lightning-strike fires. Initial Attack crews are alerted and on standby when a lightning storm is going to pass through a region. Another type of crew, Rapattack units, are three-person crews that rappel out of helicopters to fires that are hard to access due to terrain or circumstance. Project fires are visited by yet another type of crew, Unit Crews (Hotshot Crews in the United States). Unit Crews comprise 20 people, and are divided into three squads, each led by a squad boss. The entire crew is organized and run by a crew leader who answers to a variety of bosses on up the line: sector, division and fire bosses. Smoke jumper crews, wearing parachutes and a suit of armour, travel to fires by jumping out of fixed-wing aircraft. Smoke jumpers are organized in ways similar to a Unit Crew.

No matter how you get to a fire — by foot, truck, helicopter, rope, plane or boat — it's all firefighting just the same. The fireline is where the forest firefighter wants to be, and the place where we are truly in our element.

"This whole side of the fire is going off. The drop sirens from the bucketing machines are deafening as they hit spots only 15 metres away." — *Noel Hendrickson*

HUMILITY ON THE FIRELINE

by Eric T. Waters

There are occasions, working on forest fires, when you learn lessons in humility. These moments sneak up on you when you least expect them. I'm thinking about the time we were on a fire up north. I was walking down the line alone, thinking about how great life is and how cool it is to be a forest firefighter, when I came across a blown hose. I thought, *No big deal, I've done this a thousand times before*, and proceeded to try and mend it. Before I knew it, something went terribly awry and I was being sprayed in the face and in the crotch. Water went everywhere except through the hose where it was supposed to go. I was soaked, and I watched helplessly as my helmet — which was blown off in the fray — tumbled down the hill out of sight. I fixed the hose and went off in search of my helmet. Showing up without it would be most uncool.

Continuing down the line, the expression on my flush red face — not too mention my water-stained crotch — betrayed my embarrassing secret. I was forced to confess to my crewmates what had happened. At least my suffering and humiliation weren't in vain — everybody got a good laugh out of it.

One of the most humble moments during my rookie year came while we were working on the Garnet Fire of 1994 in Penticton, B.C., when one of my fellow rookies burned our squad's lunch. Several blow-ups had repeatedly threatened to jump the fire guard, so we were patrolling the green for spot-fires that the numerous sparks might ignite. It was about 3:00 p.m. and we were working up quite a hunger, but our squad boss, Mike, felt we should postpone lunch until we were sure that things had calmed down. We placed the box that contained all of our recently delivered lunches with the rest of our gear on an exposed rock outcropping, far away from any greenery on the non-burn side of the guard. Mike had us all spread out to patrol the area to look for spot-fires and put them out before they got out of hand.

After about 20 minutes, Mike, trying to keep track of all of us, yelled up to me to ask if I knew where Ken was. I looked to my right and up through the trees where I could see the orange of a hardhat worn by someone sitting on the ground. "Ken, is that you?!" After a slight delay he replied, "Yeah!" As Ken spoke, I caught a glimpse of metre-high flames through the trees immediately behind him. The sudden appearance of fire there was surreal to me — it took a few seconds for what I was looking at to register. These flames were coming from the rock outcropping that was void of trees or anything else flammable ... or so I thought.

After a few more seconds of processing, I yelled, dumbfounded, "Ken! Are those flames I see behind you?!" Ken stood up and said, "No, of course not! There's noth … *oh shit! The lunches!*" I raced through the trees toward the flame with pulaski in hand. When I finally reached the clearing, I saw Ken standing over the lone box, flames coming out of it. A single spark from the sky had floated down and landed on the box directly behind where Ken was sitting. The fire incinerated our lunches, burning nothing else.

Our squad mates heard our yelling and came running. Ken and I looked at the box, looked at each other, and had no choice but to start wailing away on our burning lunches with our pulaskis. Once the flames were doused, we hungrily sifted through the ashes to see if any food survived. The only salvageable items we could find were a few burned sandwiches covered in melted plastic, a couple of blackened apples and some now plastic-coated cookies. We all went hungry, and needless to say, Ken was not a popular guy that day.

Eric Waters, from Vancouver, has been firefighting since 1994. He works on ski patrol during the winter months and is a teacher in training.

"I do not feel as though I have to prove myself here as a woman in a male-dominated environment. I am no different from any of my other crewmates. We all have to show our strengths and contribute to the crew. Sometimes I find my actions are scrutinized differently because I am a woman; maybe my lack of aggression is taken as a lack of desire to prove myself. What I have accepted is that I cannot use the men as a benchmark from which to judge myself, especially on a physical level. My satisfaction comes from knowing that I am putting out all the effort and hard work that I am capable of — after all, work ethic and determination have nothing to do with being a man or a woman." — *Kirstine Brown*

NEVER, EVER, AND I MEAN NEVER FORGET TICKETS

by Noel Hendrickson

It's now our fifth day on the Chip Lake fire in Alberta. We love the bugless days and nights and the cool and sunny weather outside of the burn. A layer of permafrost is making dry mop-up a dream. We love our luxury trailer camps where we sleep two to a room. These rooms are warm and dry, and someone even comes in and cleans up after we leave for the day.

On this day, I wake up suddenly and realize I am running a little behind. I get to the kitchen so I can load my pack with a lunch of treats, fruit and mystery meat. What a mess I am: in one hand are my helmet, pack and saw; in the other, a coffee and an overflowing plate of eggs and toast. I'm moving full speed with laces dragging, shirt undone, bed head and aching arms. I can't be late. Passing at least three others, I make it to the bus. No disgrace, in fact some might call me a role model — an expert in time management and only slightly disheveled, with ketchup stains heralding my mastery.

Ah ... another beautiful cloudless day, ideal for patrolling. We are walking and talking, entertaining each other while we search the vast burn for hotspots. After a couple of hours we stop for a chew and snack break to be followed by the all-necessary movement. Most of us relish these bush dumps. There is just something about being naked in the woods — pale skin against the blackened earth. The break is almost over and I can feel the chewing tobacco working its magic. A ravine 30 metres south is where I take my leave. Oh, the cool breeze, the sun on my cheeks, a smooth natural seat with a luxurious backrest. Relaxation is mine ... *holy crap, I forgot T.P.!* Frantic hands, empty pockets. Options: Socks? Nope, need 'em. Underwear? Need 'em. Bandana? Hmm ... maybe. No leaves around, no smooth rocks ... wait a minute, a patch of soft moss lies under that tree. The moss works like a charm, soft and absorbent — it's a little scratchy with a few pine needles, but basically I come out of the predicament unscathed. Proud of my improvisation, I smugly pass on my knowledge to the troops. We discuss what each other would have done, and everyone has a story. I feel pretty good, but something just isn't right. My butt is really itchy and feels kind of tender. At the end of the long day of patrolling I go to my room to check my suspicions. They are confirmed with a pain I have never known. My buns are swollen and have been rubbed raw from the friction. No more quick movements: just shower and powder.

TÉMISCAMING

by David Greer

I'm in an Atco trailer in a logging and fishing camp in Témiscaming, Quebec. *Arrgghh!* Now, now, it's okay. It took two long days of travel to get here. We went from Slocan, B.C., to Vancouver by truck; to Montreal by plane; to Quebec City by plane; to Chibougamau, Quebec, by truck; to Témiscaming, Quebec, by truck, straight through — four hours of sleep, then we were on the fireline. The fire was pretty lame to start, but not today. The forest blew up rank six directly in front of us and came racing forward — a 10-storey wall of orange hell heat moving faster than I can even contemplate now. The fire came in stages; it leaped ahead in six-metre sections. It's the closest I have come to getting burned over. We ran into a lake and tried to signal some boaters, but they were too far away enjoying the show. We decided to skirt around the lake and around the fire to its backside. Wrong place, wrong time. Never again.

The bugs here are brutal. If you stop moving for even a second in these woods you'll get eaten alive. Even if you're fully protected you can go crazy from the noise and fierceness of these bloodsuckers. I cannot believe that anyone had the guts to get in a canoe and explore this region of the Canadian Shield — bugs, bog and bugs, bugs, bugs. Mozzies were flying up through the heating vents in the trailer so Mayo and I had to duct-tape them. We also duct-taped along the bottom of the door. I couldn't sleep last night because everyone was slapping the walls in their trailers, killing mozzies. It sounded like a drum circle was going on in the building, accompanied by chants of profanity. Blood splattered the walls in the morning. My blood. I don't know how they're getting in. Mayo and I went on a thorough killing spree before we went to bed — search and destroy. I hate using DEET, but at this point I'm almost willing to drink some and let it leak out my pores if only to be rid of these bloodsuckers. I'm going to breed some stingerless and suckerless mozzies for everybody to enjoy. I have to get some sleep tonight; last night, I tossed, turned and sweated like a chicken on a rotisserie.

THE LONGEST DAY

by Noel Hendrickson

It's been four hours since we refueled in Beaver Creek, Yukon, and headed back to the line of this 10-hectare fire we were sent to contain. I'm really cold tonight, and I can't stop shivering. I'm trying to dry myself with what's left of this dozing fire before it's my turn to take a two-hour shift of sleeping. In 10 minutes it will be 4:00 a.m. — time to wake the others from their damp moss beds covered with garbage-bag blankets. My boots will still be soaked when I pass out, and I know I'll feel worse when I wake up, but sleep is all I can think about. Twenty-one hours ago we were near Dawson City, extracting a machine that went down while bucketing. No one was injured, but the helicopter was sitting lame at the fire's edge, and we had to cut it out of the bush and soak it down to safeguard it. We were eating dinner when we were called out to a fire on the Yukon-Alaska border two hours southwest. It was one of the most beautiful flights I've been on, hanging low beneath the purple cotton candy sky. The past four hours of sweat and stress have gone by quicker than the last 10 minutes, but it's finally time to get some rest. I give Eric a couple kicks as he feigns sleep and finally opens his eyes. It will be another 14 hours before we're relieved and the day is over.

the myth

Fire up Thunder Creek and the mountain-
               Troy's burning!
The cloud mutters
The mountains are your mind.
The woods bristle there,
Dogs barking and children shrieking
Rise from below.
Rain falls for centuries
Soaking the loose rocks in space
Sweet rain, the fire's out
The black snag glistens in the rain
& the last wisp of smoke floats up
Into the absolute cold
Into the spiral whorls of fire
The storms of the Milky Way
"Buddha incense in an empty world"

Black pit cold and light-year
Flame tongue of the dragon
Licks the sun

The sun is but a morning star

the text

Sourdough mountain called a fire in:
Up Thunder Creek, high on a ridge.
Hiked eighteen hours, finally found
A snag and a hundred feet around on fire:
All afternoon and into night
Digging the fire line
Falling the burning snag
It fanned sparks down like shooting stars
Over the dry woods, starting spot-fires
Flaring in wind up Skagit valley
From the Sound.
Toward morning it rained.
We slept in mud and ashes,
Woke at dawn, the fire was out,
The sky was clear, we saw
The last glimmer of the morning star.

— Gary Snyder, from *Myths and Texts*

< "The Yukon is the farthest north that I've ever been. The trees are smaller here, but this 15,000-hectare fire is burning hot and taking big runs at our fuel-free. On one side, it's flanked by the Yukon River. At least the fire will stop at this massive, natural fuel-break."
— *David Greer*

> "This fire in Alberta is a giant — 180,000 hectares. Our insignificant six-kilometre section is a 40-minute helicopter flight from camp. The black-green mosaic of the burn is beneath us the entire ride. What can we possibly accomplish faced with all of this?"
— *Noel Hendrickson*

< "Twenty minutes back from the fires, jumpers are given the command to 'suit up' and a flurry of activity ensues. A reserve parachute here, a Kevlar body suit there — hard to imagine how anyone could figure out whose gear belongs to whom. Mix a little turbulence with a 30˚C aircraft interior, add 45 kilograms of gear and the exertion of suiting up, and you get a steady flow of sweat. After a complete equipment check, each jumper takes a seat on the floor and anxiously waits for the removal of the inflight door. Whoosh ... close your eyes as every dust and sand particle is whipped into a violent tornado and sucked out the open door — cool relief for sweat-soaked jumpers." — *Pete Laing*

> "The view from the aircraft was surreal: jumpers in the air, helicopters working fires six kilometres away, air tankers dropping retardant on fires 12 kilometres away, all the while huge columns of smoke pushed up into the troposphere along the horizon. It was like a war zone in there. The empty DC3 arrived in Whitehorse 12 hours after leaving that morning. During the course of the day the plane refueled four times, 10 jumpers were deployed on three separate fires and more than 1,350 kilograms of cargo was dropped." — *Pete Laing*

"We have no water, so we're doing old-time firefighting here tonight. I have been digging and smudging hotspots for the past nine hours, yet I'm still driven. I like getting so close to this earth and heat. We're working in pairs — one pulaski to slash through the duff to the soil and one shoveler to throw the sweet dirt on the fire, keeping the flames out of the canopy."
— *David Greer*

< "The helipad that we started two days ago is now burned over. Hot fire ripped through our pad and over our guard, and kept going. Lonely, defeated helipad."
— *David Greer*

> "We cut a road around the fire using chainsaws and bodies to clear the trees and brush. This way the fire will run out of fuel once it burns up to the edge of the fuel-free." — *David Greer*

< I executed some of the best guard digging of my career, clean and deep. I was swamping with Ed while Colin sawed. You can get into amazing shape doing this job hard for a lot of days. When you can stop and sit down at the end of the day, and it's sunny and clear, it's so right. I think about sex, music and food, in that order."
— *David Greer*

"They didn't teach us how to get through this slop,
> loaded down with hoses, at the official ATV-certification course. The melting permafrost has turned the Cat guard into a gummy pool of muck more than one metre deep in spots. I'm in one of them, waiting for the Cat to tow me out. I can barely see over the 10 lengths of hose strapped to the front of the quad and the pumps tied to the rear keep digging into my back. I've long since been painted head to toe, and now the mud is drying and peeling off my face and arms. This truly is the life — mud pies at age 28." — *Noel Hendrickson*

< "I like meeting people from the region where we're fighting fire. They understand the area and the situation — it is their situation. For them, the stakes are much higher. They're usually local loggers who are called upon to help fight the fire. Our first meetings are usually uncomfortable for them since we're a different breed of bush people, or so it seems at first glance. In our crew, we all wear uniforms and, for the most part, come from the city, yet we all have a common topic or two: cars, sports, working in the bush. They love to hear about our pranks, and I think they enjoy the camaraderie that we take for granted most of the time." — *David Greer*

> "The burn cuts distinct lines into the green in distant hillsides. I store these memories away in my mind as if in a scrapbook: turning over soil and ashpits, digging up moss, fuel-free cutting patterns around the burn, and the dreamy blue sky — clouds locked into still life." — *David Greer*

"We're in an unbelievable spot. There are burned-out snags everywhere. Yesterday a vole climbed all over me after I had inadvertently sprayed him — he broke my heart as he waddled away after I put him down."
— *David Greer*

"The sun has just come out and now it's time for chewing and patrolling. I have a nice view here. I hope that we patrol in squads, as this is a small territory with little smoke. Some stress is building as the end of this fire is near, and it will be time for travel arrangements. I need some time out with my girl for relationship control. I hope my letters reached her." — *David Greer*

< "The only way to put out a fire is with pulaskis ... It's the firefighter swinging the pulaski that puts out the fire."
— Jim Dunlop

> "If I didn't know any better I would marvel at how beautiful that bright red plume of retardant is. Unfortunately, I know the messy truth — the planes drop it right where we have to work. The fireline becomes a slippery, frothy skating rink of red fertilizer. This muck stains your boots and clothes, burns your skin and gets into the sweat that stings your eyes."
— *Noel Hendrickson*

< "I can remember going through a tunnel on one fire that was part flame, part smoke. I had about 12 guys and I told them not to run, just walk. They said "to hell with it," and started to run, and so did I. If there had been an Olympics that year those 12 guys and I would have won any running event." — *Jim Dunlop*

> "It's hard to breathe and see in here. The machines are constantly bucketing to help us control the flare-ups. We're on our radios competing for air support, since there's only one machine for us right now. I'm exhausted as we've been trying to punch this line in before the fire takes a run. If it does we'll have to get out quick, likely losing our line." — *David Greer*

< "We're working to save a heritage site near Dawson City that contains old trapper cabins. The folk who live and work here are terrified as the fire moves closer. The whole crew feels confident, if not cocky, that we'll put the fire down, but there's no way of conveying this to the residents, no way to comfort them. They haven't been in the middle of a firestorm before." — *David Greer*

> "The monotony of hosing and mop-up drag on for weeks. We work in pairs, exchanging stories and conundrums to amuse each another. We search the area for ashpits that hiss like sauna rocks when they're sprayed. We look forward to chew breaks, snacks, lunches, flare-ups ... anything to make the 12 hours at the end of the hose pass a little quicker." — *Noel Hendrickson*

< "We're trekking through moose country, past smouldering piles of droppings, antlers and skulls, but still I haven't seen a single moose in the past week. We're searching for a burning squirrel cache that will burn for the next 40 years unless we find it. The black flies keep taking big chunks of my skin. I ask myself whether this is worse than day 12 on the last fire on that 90-degree slope of slide alder with 18 rolls of econoline hose stuffed in my shirt, a pulaski, a leaky can of gas, and four lengths of inch-and-a-half hose, when I lost my balance, reached out, and grabbed a big fist of devil's club just before I went sprawling down the ravine." — *Geraldine Woods*

> "Today I saw one of the saddest things I've ever seen on the fireline. We found a nest in a tree that was just felled. The naked baby birds were falling out — awkward and helpless. Andrew picked them up and put them back in their nest, but we knew that the mother was not going to come back. Later that day, on our way back through, we came across the nest again and one chick had died or was dying and the other two were struggling. Noah had to turn his head as he mercifully stomped the nest with his boot. Kelly turned away and could not look — nobody talked or mentioned it again for the rest of the day." — *David Greer*

< "During forest fires animals are displaced, singed and sometimes burned to death. The fire flushes them out of the forest: deer, rabbits, shrews, voles, skunks, porcupines .... Sometimes we find abandoned babies and nests but there's little we can do." — *Noel Hendrickson*

> "Some people are very quiet and don't like to talk about their past. Others are quiet because they've snapped mentally — they're 'done.' This job comes down to mental toughness, and the ability to work hard physically — keeping emotions in check. Once your physical endurance is exhausted and your mental state deteriorates, your body is useless." — *David Greer*

< "Rainy wet brush walk day. My feet are like two flat red tomatoes and they hurt just as much, no powder is effective. I'm out here hitting hotspots — thinking about Emily Carr for some reason." — *David Greer*

> "It's good to tune out occasionally to maintain sanity — even if it's only for a few minutes. This morning one of the giant burned-out cedars collapsed and smashed down in the middle of our squad. One crew member dived out of the way — his helmet flew off and luckily was the only thing squashed. In moments such as these, the water drowns out the sounds of the fire. The droning pumps, buzzing saws and whapping helicopters fade away." — *Noel Hendrickson*

"High ground at last. These new boots are still stiff, bought three weeks ago, back when the blisters started. Those days of hiking Alberta's north in May: days of thawing permafrost and heel-tearing gumbo. Days of 'sippi' mud holes and 12-hour patrols. My feet didn't breath very well with the duct tape around them, but it was the only thing that didn't come off when they were soaked and swollen." — *Noel Hendrickson*

< "Machines and nature — machines mimicking nature. Even helicopters are beautiful in this environment, somehow plunking down beside us with insect precision. Even though this place is spectacular, it's difficult to enjoy these surroundings since I'll soon be taken to that ugly fireline." — *David Greer*

> "The trees are huge in here. Allan, Mitch and Noel are up ahead of us taking down the snags and the nasty flaming ones. From a mile away I can hear these bad boys lifting the earth, crashing headlong down the steep slope and hitting the ground, taking down everything in their path, until they finally hit the river, where they drop in and go for a ride." — *David Greer*

"On our last day in Yukon, the hose is all pulled and rolled. Eighty lengths in all: econo, thiefs, three-ways, nozzles; pulaskis stuck in stumps. We are waiting for our ride out of here, trying to keep the mozzies at bay, after having endured 14 days. The fire is quiet and everybody is done. There are no helicopters or chainsaws buzzing, no smoke, just a clear surreal view of the mountains and hills of Dawson City." — *David Greer*

"We spent three days swamping and cutting a fuel-free in Atlin, B.C. Our camp is in the middle of nowhere, where it's so cold in the mornings that I have been doing push-ups to stay warm while waiting for our ride at the helipad." — *David Greer*

"From the boat I can see the rest of the crew moving up the slope trying to get a handle on this now-lazy fire that nearly overran the wilderness lodge we were there to protect. The three of us are motoring down the milky Yukon River, charged with the task of protecting an old cabin that is in the path of the massive blaze. There's nothing like an adventure — a boating adventure, no less — to break up the monotony of a long fire like this one. This is a dream; the absolute freedom of the river, the fresh air and loving sun, I want it all to last. We finish setting up the sprinkler system to protect the cabin, then sprawl out on the sandbar where the helicopter is going to pick us up. I take it all in knowing full well what awaits us back at camp. The crew will be pissed off, since we escaped the madness for the day and they didn't, and they're going to let us know it." — *Noel Hendrickson*

< "Sunlight and swamped wood. Charlie makes a game out of lifting logs — adding some fun to pass 12 hours of hard work, establishing fun and teamwork ... putting the shoulder into it ... feeling the balance without falling backward ... some impressive lifts. Giving people tasks to complete. Politics as to who your boss is — the bosses bonding together to help make things go smoothly. Every day, everybody gets wearier. Inner conflicts turn into outbursts. Talking, arguing about small things — that are hiding the bigger issues." — *David Greer*

> "From the ridge I take photos of my evacuating peers against a backdrop of the Yukon River and the 40,000-hectare fire that is closing in around us. My radio continues to squawk — something about getting my butt down to the helipad. The whole scene is compelling, warlike, a feast for the senses that draws me nearer and forces an awe-inspired smile across my soot-black face. Grinning like some kind of madman, I spin around to see a helicopter hovering over the cliff at eye level behind me. The pilot shakes his head disapprovingly and not so politely motions for me to make my way down to the river for pick up." — *Noel Hendrickson*

"Though we walk in silence, not saying a word, the air is filled with the sounds of scorched moss and twigs crunching underfoot, and the creak of rootless trees we push over, our tools clanging against what is left. We are assembled in a row of 20, covering miles of bog. A chorus of suctioned slurps reminds us of the blisters on our heels. There's always a whiner among us who ends the silence — this time it's not me. The griper makes us all feel better about ourselves, stronger, and smugly superior. United, we 19 mock the whiner, thankful that he gave in before we did. Now the group has a scapegoat, and laughter resumes. No longer bored, sore or alone with our thoughts, we hike searching for signs of smoke, feeling the earth for hotspots." — *Noel Hendrickson*

SALMON ARM — A CASE STUDY

THE SITUATION

by David Greer

The fire was started by a lightning strike on Fly Hills. It has grown to about 50 hectares by the time we arrive. The forest in this particular region is ripe for burning: its floor is littered with fallen snags, twigs, thick underbrush and deep dry duff. It's difficult to take a single step in here without tripping over something. Fires have been suppressed here for years, and the fuels have built up. Fire is a natural process and it serves to eliminate buildup by burning the underbrush and the dead dry matter on the ground. This forest has been waiting and wanting to burn. But it's Catch-22 because when a fire starts near a community, it is, of course, necessary to suppress it. We can see the fire burning up on the hill when we drive into town. In fact, we can see three separate fires burning on the mountains surrounding Salmon Arm. Water tankers and helicopters are dropping water on the Fly Hills fire, but it's burning down much deeper than the treetops. The ground is on fire and the water is just not getting through the thick brush.

We try to lay some hose around some of the hottest parts of the fire, and we attempt to line-locate for more Cat guard in order to extend our control line. Colin and Mike are line-locating up ahead of the crew. The wind really starts to pick up: all I can hear is the violent snapping and popping from the fire up ahead — it sounds like a red hot frying pan filled with sizzling oil. Colin and Mike retreat out of the woods when they sense the fury advancing upon them. The Martin Mars water bomber is called in to cool our area, but the relief is temporary since the hulking airplane can only slow the fire, not put it out. Even with the hose laid up near the fire we can't get enough water up the hill to even charge the hose. There's no water source close to us so we have to rely on too few water trucks that have to drive back down the hill to reload. It reaches a point where we have to evacuate the heavy equipment. It's crucial to leave them enough time to get out of there if the fire really takes off.

A short time later we're sent running. We pull our hose back as far and as quick as we can and hightail it out of there. We meet up with all of the operators and their equipment at the staging area and watch helplessly as the water bombers and helicopters try to get close enough to drop water on the huge, billowing mushroom cloud. The pilots are risking their lives in there. They are narrowly avoiding one another as they navigate through the smoke. The wind from the firestorm is tossing the aircraft around like kites. They look like paper airplanes fluttering around as they try to get closer to this massive conflagration. When it looks like our escape routes could become compromised, we have to evacuate the mountain altogether. We arrive back at our base defeated, feeling useless and unworthy. The next day is much the same, and the fire just keeps growing.

On our third day the fire really goes off. Winds howling up to 145-kilometres-per-hour kick up the flames to demonic proportions as they spread to the valley below, then proceed to rip up the other side. We jump in our trucks and race down the mountain and into the valley so we can help curtail the destruction. I'm listening to the frightening developments on my radio as it all goes down. Jim Mottishaw, the fire boss, is in a helicopter over the Salmon River valley, giving instructions to the people on the ground below. He's directing Cats to dig guard around structures and houses, and instructing personnel on the ground to set up sprinkler systems on top of houses and to brace themselves for the firestorm. I hear that first defining call, "Jim, there are a couple of barns going up over here on Branchflower Road."

We pass the camp on our way into the valley. Our ranger tents have been blown over by the winds and our beds, sleeping bags and personal gear litter the camp. We struggle to stand up against the wind when we leap out of the trucks to lend a hand to the overmatched camp crew. We drive into the worst hit areas of the valley and work on saving buildings that have a chance for survival. Meanwhile, the fire is tearing up Mount Ida, kicking up 100-metre flames — the valley is a war zone. Helicopters and planes fly everywhere, dropping retardant on houses and property that are in danger of being engulfed. Fire trucks and police cars drive up and down the roads with their lights flashing. The fire on the valley hills looks like a rippling orange blanket — it starts to resemble flowing lava when night falls.

We have no time to assess the situation; we just do what we can wherever we are. Firefighters run from house to house with pulaskis and hoses, desperately looking for water. It's so frustrating to search and find no water; all the water systems run on electricity, and hydro had to shut down the power lines because they, too, were burning. We end up pumping water out of anything we can — hot tubs, troughs. We work through the night without resting. The plan is for us to sleep a few hours at the Rapattack base. In the three hours we have been allotted for sleep, we end up searching for our gear that has been thrown into several trucks back at our wind-torn camp. It's all mixed together — one shoe here, one shoe there. I can't find my sleeping bag so I just sleep on the unforgiving linoleum-covered concrete floor. No one can sleep (except, perhaps, the walrus — Noel). With rest period over, we lift our sore backs and bodies off that sinister floor and drive back to the valley. The fire is now estimated at 3,000 hectares and growing, and I am on an adrenaline and sleep-deprivation high.

In the days that follow, another windstorm is predicted; more people are evacuated from Salmon Arm and a provincial state of emergency is called. Everyone is cagey on the eve of the windstorm.

"We're on standby right now as the Martin Mars water bomber actions this place. I heard it before I saw it. I knew it was coming, but I'm still shocked to see this hulking giant skimming the treetops directly overhead. It sounds like a war." — *David Greer*

"We've been evacuated for the second day in a row. Waiting, pacing, feeling useless as the fire takes a firm hold on the west side of the valley." — *Noel Hendrickson*

Only a few of us can sleep. It is during times like this that I cherish the closeness of our crew — we are sleeping 10 to a tent, side by side. We sleep on foamies and each have about a foot of personal space on either side of us. Someone else's stinky socks become your stinky socks when your limited airspace is assaulted.

The wind is howling, but we're prepared for it. We've roped and nailed down our ranger tents, and this time they're not caving in. Yet all I can do is lie on my back and watch the roof of the tent ripple. Fortunately, by morning, the storm dies down. Now we gather at the trucks for a briefing; we know that this is our opportunity to get a handle on this thing. The fire has stalled at the top of Mount Ida and is threatening to rip down into Salmon Arm. We make our way up the mountain and start our advance on the fire's perimeter. We wait all day for favourable conditions so we can burn off. We are able to burn off small areas throughout the morning and afternoon, but we have to be extremely cautious at this crucial point of the day, so we bide our time until dark.

Finally, the night comes and the conditions are perfect. We load up the trucks with fuel, hoses, tools and drip torches, then drive through the valley and up Mount Ida. Skidders and water trucks accompany us for support. We're excited and scared as we ponder what will happen if our plan goes awry. I think about the people of Salmon Arm sleeping down below and what they would think if they knew that we were about to light up the forest that has caused them so much grief and worry. We're all feeling tense, as there is no margin for error. We spread out along our control line and start to light up some test patches. It looks good, so we start to light up larger tracts of land. The flames shoot up into the trees and into the sky. It's a beautiful sight — every spark can be seen flying in the night sky like fireflies. The forest turns a bright orange-red and reflects on our expressions of pyromaniacal glee. We become jubilant knowing that we have succeeded; the main fire no longer has any fuel to look forward too. We have starved it by spoiling its food. I wonder if anyone down below noticed.

In the following days, we have to make sure that we do not lose the advantage we have gained over our foe. We put in long hours so that we can cool down as much of the fire's perimeter as possible. We advance farther every day, slowly choking out the fire. We remain methodical in our task, working the edges and going in deeper every day. We will be in Salmon Arm for 26 days before the mop-up of this fire is complete. When we leave, other crews will rotate in as mop-up of this enormous blaze continues well into the winter. The fire is scanned every day with infrared, and hotspots are flagged to ensure every last spot is located and extinguished. The scan is so fine-tuned that it can pick up the heat from a smouldering cigarette butt. When we finally get back to base camp, I'll go home to Vancouver for two days, and when I come back, we'll pack up our gear and head to Revelstoke, B.C., for another fire.

SALMON ARM — THE WORK

by David Greer

I'm in Salmon Arm on a skid trail with two pumpkins and a pump. The last two days have been mad with wildfire and windstorms. Energy of this nature influences us all. This is an interface fire — we have been fighting fire in the suburbs, in backyards — empty houses and spot-fire war zones everywhere. Some people have lost everything, and some will never know just how close they were. They will never know that I was on their roof, stamping out sparks and starts. I was in their kitchen turning on their taps to see if I could get a little water. They didn't hear me swear, turn around and tromp out.

I dug up your cedar-shake roof with my pulaski. I climbed your drainpipe and bent your gutters as I made my way up there. It was messy. You may have been sleeping — or lying awake — in the community centre, a motel or at the home of a friend or family member. It was dark by the time I got to your house; the power was out and your water pump system was on electric. I dug up some spots in your front yard while some of my squad mates went behind your house to cut down trees that were burning or were going to burn and were draping over your eaves. I knew that you would understand. I felt guilty about all of the houses that we had to leave to burn because it was too late to save them. We only tried to save the ones we had a good chance of saving. Some houses were already consumed or about to be. When I left your house I thought of leaving you a note, but I didn't have time, and I didn't know how you would feel.

We try to make calm and rational decisions about which houses to save and which ones to let go. I'm always looking over my shoulder at the houses across the street that we leave behind. I want to go over there but I have to focus on the property I'm working on. We all want to save every house, but when rational thinking prevails over our emotions, we keep our minds on the task at hand. I keep thinking about the people who live in the neighbourhood we're in. I'm trying to picture the people who live here. I wonder what their reactions will be when they arrive home to find their house destroyed, or to find it saved and still intact, but everything around it scorched.

This fire is shocking and it shows on the grim-looking, tear-strewn faces of my peers. We cannot believe it — the fire is such an amazing sight. Yet we are all disturbed by its dark and menacing presence. It is an eerie feeling — I struggle to find the right words to describe it. It is a complete mind and body experience — the fire sucks out of you every possible sensation, every feeling you never knew you had or experienced, just like the fire draws the oxygen out of the air that it consumes. It is frenetic and exhilarating. Your fight-or-flight instinct kicks in hard, and your central nervous system does not know what to do, yet it struggles to stay centred. Adrenaline takes over and

< "I love the mystery of this evening burn-off — the shadows of people and flame bending and moving together — drip torches gleaming in blackened hands, like some kind of primitive weapon. It's harder for this fire to hide, as every flicker of orange gives it away."
— *David Greer*

you forget how tired you are even though it is hard to focus on one task because you want to do everything at once.

I'm surprised by how everyone reacts at different times during the long night. I notice how calm I am compared to the rookies and others who have not seen such aggressive fire activity. I have experienced this type of over-stimulus before — the energy that the powerful force of a natural disaster brings. In my rookie year, I experienced a similar situation in Penticton, B.C., at the Garnet Fire in 1994. People lost their homes in that inferno as well. As a rookie, I really did not understand what was going on. I did what I was told to do and watched the veterans for their reactions. I stepped back and took it all in. Salmon Arm is different for me because I know what can happen and what is going to happen. I know that the strange feeling I get before all hell breaks loose is not to be ignored.

The sky and the sun turn a peculiar colour before it happens. You notice it right away; even if you don't know what is going to happen or have never before experienced wildfire. A strange orange colour fills the sky and clings to the sun. You start to check everyone's position. You assess your escape routes, pick the best one and start heading toward it. You get out now.

Up to this point, during the entire previous working day, you really truly feel that you can win. No doubt enters your mind. You figure that all you have to do is the right things at the right time and you can win.

I feel really guilty because of the excitement I've been experiencing from the time we got the fire call. Everything that I have trained for and experienced during the past five years has prepared me for this moment. I know that this is the one. I am so confident with my skills and knowledge. I get excited when my crew gets a fire call, we all do. I get called upon to do my job, my work. I train hard all year long. Rainy nights running up and down hills, going to the gym when some days I don't really feel like it. I put in the hours. I am motivated to perform for the fire season and I think about it every day.

When people ask me how my fire season was, I respond depending on the number of fire days I've had. It is a good season if I see a lot of fire, and a bad season if it rains too much. Unless I'm fighting fire I do not really feel as if I'm doing my job. Do paramedics feel the same way?

"Evacuation, Salmon Arm. You know when you're defeated. There's no shame, only dejection because of all the hard work done, now lost. It's strange and sad watching the heavy equipment awkwardly trying to escape — the machines themselves look as if they feel shame. At times like these, I try to remind myself that fire is a natural phenomenon and preventing it is not."
— *David Greer*

"The windstorm blew a lot of tents over in our camp last night. Plywood platforms flew around like sheets of paper, flipping end over end. Meanwhile, the fire continues to flare up on the mountain, sending a message for all to see. Beneath it all, we're camped on someone's ranch, fighting fires in the backyards of mansions, our tents collapsed." — *David Greer*

< "Dust from the Cat guard is coating my body and lungs, and is beginning to pile up in the corners of my eyes. Silt and sand grinding between my teeth, I can taste the Okanagan on my muddied tongue. This fire in Salmon Arm reminds me of the Garnet Fire of 1994 in Penticton, B.C., a similar fire, a similar cat guard but there the silt was knee-deep, like wading through warm talcum powder. It took a month to get that fire out of my lungs, even longer to sweat the grime out of my pores." — *Noel Hendrickson*

> "The heat from active ground fire is indescribable. It is about 39°C out here today and the combination is nearly unbearable. I am running in with hose and pulaski at intervals, so I don't burn or overheat. My uniform is glued to my body and the ground is melting my boot soles." — *David Greer*

> "The predicted windstorm is throwing our ranger tent around, and I doubt my friends inside are sleeping. I sit down and watch the fire flare up on the mountainside, clearly visible from our vantage point in the valley. The sky is strangely lit — not like city lights lighting up the surrounding land, but like a hot fire burning and licking up into the sky with every gust. The energy of a natural disaster is incredible. All the flickering makes me tremble with indescribable excitement. I'm scared in anticipation of tomorrow, yet excited and honoured to be here." — *David Greer*

< "We can see the smoke twist across the burning valley as we approach. The evacuating farm trucks loaded with livestock or keepsakes and valuables warned us of what was to come but didn't fully prepare us for what was hidden farther down the valley. As we speed past the last evacuee and into the twilight, a quiet anxiety comes over us. The flames dance over the valley floor, leaving farmsteads razed to the ground. While passing these still-standing homes, a plea is voiced by each of us in the crew cab: 'That yellow one is on fire....' 'What about that one with the swing set in the front yard....' 'Hey, there's someone running out to the road from that one....' I couldn't stop wondering if we'd chosen the right homes to save. Who are we to decide anyway?" — *Noel Hendrickson*

"Initially I thought someone had turned a light on in the hay barn, but the light just keeps getting brighter; then come the flames. I slump to the ground and watch as the whole thing is consumed in minutes. It is as mesmerising as a campfire. Ignited strands of hay fly from the barn. The metal ceiling melts and is half torn away before I open my ears again and hear the thunderous crashing of the roof in the wind. It sounds like an empty freight train rolling by a car window as you wait to cross the tracks. Could I have done anything to save that barn? Guilt weighs down on me as I wonder what I would have risked had that been my barn. Yet we could do nothing but sit in that field of dry grass with our ears pounding and our bloodshot eyes burning. We could not control that force, whose power is terrifying and beautiful. It's something you can't take your eyes off." — *Noel Hendrickson*

"Shawn and Melissa Wiebe were not among the families spared from losing their homes. The couple, who have not yet celebrated their first anniversary, returned to their rented house in Silver Creek to find it burned to the ground.... Now, they sit in the lobby of their new home — a hotel room of the McGuire Inn. They are remarkably level-headed about their experience and speak more often about their misfortune. 'If it were five minutes later we would have all been dead.' They show pictures of their flight from Silver Creek — incredible shots of the fire moving down the mountain as they fled with one last load of belongings. 'There was debris falling on us when we left,' she said, adding the state of her neighbourhood was also frightening. 'You could see the panic all over,' she said." — *Heather Persson*, Salmon Arm Observer, 12 August 1998

"It's hard to believe this stand was spitting ash and flame into the valley only four days earlier. Almost all of this forest in the valley appeared the same: burned clean from the intense heat of Wednesday night. It surprised me that the charred land seemed so beautiful. It had been cleansed and now reborn, silent and vulnerable." — *Noel Hendrickson*

< "At last the winds have turned in our favour and we can burn off this draw that has been such a nuisance over the last few days. It's a rush to release so much energy, to hear that low rumble of wind and flames. It feels good not to fight it this time." — *Noel Hendrickson*

> "I'm on my way back to camp roaming this desolate place beneath the five o'clock shadow of the valley, nearly seven months after the Salmon Arm fire was put to bed. The creeks are thick with ash and debris — it will be a long time before the scars heal. I've been looking for a section of guard that I recognise or a pocket of green that we saved from the fire. Nothing looks the same. There are just charred poles and freshly cut stumps." — *Noel Hendrickson*

END OF SEASON

Noel,

I can't explain the response or my feelings adequately enough after I was injured. My back was broken while fighting a wildfire a few years ago, leaving me paralyzed below the waist. Even after five seasons, I expected the people from my base to support me the most, but the support of everyone else has overwhelmed my fellow crewmembers and me.

I received cards, letters, phone calls, faxes, fruit baskets, T-shirts, photographs, gifts, not just addressed to me, but to my family, my crew and my base. All of this happened immediately, and it continued for a number of months — long after the fire season ended. Their support hasn't stopped to this day. It wasn't what they sent, but what they said and why they did it that meant the most. All of them put in the time and energy to do these things — as my mom has said to me, "That has meant everything."

To sum it up, especially to sum up what wildland firefighting has meant to me, it is this esprit de corps that overwhelms me. With the friendships and bonds I've made through wildfire — people I consider now to be my sisters and brothers — I don't know if I could ever give them up if it meant never fighting fire in the first place and never getting injured.

Wildfire created so much of me, of who I am, my passions and my friends. Firefighting has practically been a rite of passage for me. My gift to everyone in return for their undying loyalty and love is to show them all how short and precious life can be; that things can change so quickly; to live life as positively as they can; and to let them know how grateful I feel to be able to still say: "Thank you for everything."

Brad Hartley

Brad Hartley worked as an Initial Attack firefighter for BCFS and is now a safety consultant. He wrote this letter to Noel when asked if he would contribute to this book.

FALL FIRE

by David Greer

Although I can sense it days before it happens, fire season always seems to end abruptly. My senses are so in tune with my surroundings that each and every slight change in temperature, light and humidity is fully comprehended. My nose and skin pick up the fall air the second it blows in. I get to a point in the woods where I can smell someone coming, and sometimes I even know who it is. In the fall, fire tries to hide in the bright orange and red leaves. It no longer finds such willing allies in the sun and air. Shorter days and the ever-increasing evening chill start to slow the fire's activity. Dew lingers on a fall day and dew point becomes fire's biggest foe. When fall starts to tighten its grip, I start to think about going back to school. The changing and falling of the leaves trigger these feelings.

But this is the first year I will not be returning to school. I now linger a little longer on the fireline. In the first weeks of September I watch our student corps leave for school, watch them fall away like leaves. I remember a fire in Ontario in my second season. September was upon us and school was calling, yet I was resisting because I was just getting so comfortable out there. It was already two weeks into classes and I was at the stage where I could be crossed off the class list at any moment and left to enrol in obscure courses with names like "The Inner Child and Peculiar Habits of the North Austrian Rodent." I finally accepted the fact that fire season was over for me, so I caved in and declined a further extension.

We were scheduled to leave our line camp Monday morning, so timing was going to be crucial if I wanted to get back to my 8:30 a.m. class on Tuesday, and logistics are rarely on my side. About five of us were leaving that day, and about 10 souls were staying behind. It was strange and painful to see those guys gearing up for a day on the line — I had already turned that switch off. I could almost feel my first hot shower and taste the pizza and sushi that awaited me back in the city. A group of us were lifted out of our line camp by helicopter and taken to base camp near Chapleau, Ontario. There was some downtime at the camp, so I decided to oil up my dry boots and make them handsome again. This job is religious for me. My boot oil is like incense to my nose and its application is as careful, dedicated and crucial as a Japanese tea ceremony. I sat in a perfect spot by the lake in the comforting sun and concentrated on my peaceful task.

Our bus finally arrived and we boarded for a long, bumpy and dusty trip into Chapleau. We stopped there for breakfast and then carried on to Thunder Bay. From there we boarded a plane for Castlegar, B.C., with lengthy stopovers in Saskatoon and Kamloops. Picking up one of our trucks in Castlegar, we drove to our base camp in Slocan. It was already dark when I went into my tent and hurriedly packed all the crap I thought I was going to need that summer into large black garbage

"When fall starts to tighten its grip, I start to think about going back to school. The changing and falling of the leaves trigger these feelings." — *David Greer*

bags (the quickest, messiest technique and the most likely way to lose something). I threw the bags into my van, said goodbye to everyone and peeled out of camp.

I had an eight-and-a-half hour night drive ahead of me, so I decided to relieve my boredom by chewing the last of my tobacco and by drinking bad road coffee. I savoured my last dip because it was going to be my last until the next season on the fireline. The small towns along the Crowsnest Highway flashed by in the night and I rolled down my window to smell the different landscapes along my route. It was around 6:00 a.m. when city lights were finally upon me. I drove up to Simon Fraser University and had about two and a half hours before my Shakespeare class. I slept uneasily in the parking lot and upon waking I rummaged through my bags and picked out some clothes that had not become saturated with smoke. I threw them on and headed off to the gym showers for a good scrubbing. Leaving a blackened shower stall, I dried my long hair and scruffy beard and headed off to class. I arrived on time and in shock as I had not seen so many clean and civilized people in one place for quite some time. I guess I couldn't belch out loud anymore, and I would have to get reacquainted with toilets again.

Twenty-four hours from the fireline, no sleep, thrust back into civilization and academia — my head was reeling. I introduced myself to my professor; he eyed me suspiciously. The comforting smell of the lecture theatre with all its wood panelling and seats was a familiar pleasure to my senses. I almost felt guilty to be able to enjoy such luxury. I shuffled off to the least inhabited region of the theatre and tucked myself into the back corner. As I looked out over the heads of my fellow students, I self-righteously thought to myself: *You people have no idea where I was 24 hours ago — you could never imagine.* I mean, I still had a bit of trench foot from walking around in all that swamp muck. *Man, it's hot in here ... not used to the inside.* I had literally crawled out of the woods like the missing link. I flinched as I thought of my mates in Ontario in the midst of their morning patrol. I was so hot that I started to sweat, my hands started to leak black as my pores opened up. My notepaper quickly became smudged with soot. It would be a few days before I got it all out of my system. My skin looked like it had tiny little blackheads all over it. I swear some people were giving me some weird looks, like I was some kind of beast or something. I felt other students eyeballing me, and I thought I heard someone mutter to a friend "Have you seen that movie, *Quest for Fire?*" The student closest to me caught a whiff and shifted in his seat uneasily. He became anxious, as if he'd heard the fire alarm.

> "Last day here — we are bugging out. Had a nice sauna in our drying tent last night — everyone in a good mood. Back to civilization. I can't wait to wash. It's hard to believe that I could be in class by Tuesday 8:00 a.m. These boots will be clean and mean to some in the city. I have to remember how beautifully the trees reflected off the water here at sunset. I will remember all these characters in their scenes." — *David Greer*

Dear Mike,

I'm supposed to be writing a paper right now, but as Kendahl and I are in the process of moving, I happened to stumble upon my cache of photo albums. I've been feeling funny for awhile now about the changes going on in my life. Funny in a good way, though. I guess because my feelings take me away to another time and place. That place is the Kootenays; the time is the last seven years. The photo albums are like chronological "days in the life." They document first fires, old girlfriends, the young faces of old friends and mornings of nothing but freedom to look forward to. Letting go is much more difficult than I thought it would be. So much of my life has been influenced by forest firefighting. Sometimes I wonder if anybody else can really understand how much it all means to me. You do, though, and the crew. Allow me to be sentimental when I say that I'm going to miss it all, every goddamn thing. My eyes are a little misty right now. I have a hankering for the jukebox at Sam's, a stroll to the river, a drive up the valley with a beer between my legs, the window down, a wild night in Nelson, a lazy Sunday and the smell from the top of a fire all at once. It's good to feel strongly about things, even if it hurts a little. For me, every memory brings at least a shake of the head, if not a shit-eating grin to my face. Please spill a little beer in the river and say my name, so the Slocan knows that I haven't abandoned her, I'm just doing some exploring and I will be back soon.

I wish you and the crew all the best Mike. I'll be thinking of you guys.

Love,

Tim (Tadpole)

Tim Pulfrey worked as a firefighter from 1992 to 1998. He is presently employed as an outpost nurse in the Queen Charlotte Islands. He sent this letter the year he retired, to his crew leader, Mike Allan.

BIG SWAN HILLS DIP — Thursday, May 21, 1998
by David Greer

Orange peels on the ground, horsetails all around. Big chew in the lip.

Playing like boys do when they pretend they are men.

Firemen playing, working hard, then playing — chewing tobacco, spitting, talking on our radios.

Real things this time.

Squeezed orange peel rind and rubbed on wrists, flying in helicopters — rubbing it in.

Smelling for smoke and swinging the pulaski — digging with the shovel — dreaming of girls

and some fine things.

Black soot on white body — ground in, not easily removed — kicking logs with leather boots.

Thinking of Gary Snyder. Old enough to know better

and not old enough to commit to not playing in the woods every summer

sleeping in cold tents — cold nights sleeping in your days-old clothes,

which turn into more days — keeping your mind and thoughts and feelings in check.

Horsetails   grow   in   sections   they pull   apart, but are easily put backtogether.

Mel the skidder driver worked in the Queen Charlottes like my dad and other friends' dads.

Chewing tobacco he says, "You can hit the eye of a snake at 100 yards." I believe him.

I think of the north-northwest coast and the west coast of the island.

Travelling throughout the year.

Mud everywhere and only the mind for entertainment, as you do your own thing.

Staying warm. Staying cool — accepting sweat and chills — keeping your sentimental gear.

Keeping a tight kit. Remembering other fires and they end the same — with relief and reflection. Working to

stimulate the mind, singing out songs and still in my prime.

Graphite on paper, charcoal on my clothes. The burn meets the green. Meeting old friends on

the fireline — other crews that you know.

They all end the season and go to exotic places, or they go to work in more mud.

The burn, the mud, the blue sky, the green. Wearing the same clothes every day.

Same food, different people playing, working, sleeping, sharing every day.

Nelson and its mellow thing tucked in the southeast corner

I dream.

air tanker

GLOSSARY

The glossary includes definitions necessary for the reader to understand some of the language and terminology found in the text. Some unnecessary definitions are also included strictly for our own, and hopefully your, amusement.

AID: aerial ignition device. Flaming balls of gel shot from helicopters to ignite forest in a burn-off situation.

air tanker: airplane that carries between 2,700 and 27,000 litres of water or retardant. Also known as water bombers. *See also* Martin Mars.

backcheck valve: used in water delivery to prevent water from flowing out of the pump (losing prime) during pump shutdown or breakdown.

back-firing: method of indirect attack used in extreme situations with fast-moving or inaccessible fires that cannot be contained. The control line is established well ahead of the main fire. The intervening fuel is burned off with the aid of convection winds to establish as wide a strip as possible before the main fire front arrives at the control line.

banana roll: a stick approximately one metre long is used to roll hose into a banana-shaped roll. A method used primarily in the bush to pull or move hose, and a necessary skill for any self-respecting firefighter.

banana suit: bright yellow jumpsuits given to rookies during their first week at camp.

bird dog: lead plane in an air tanker convoy, which establishes the bombing pattern to be followed.

blow-up: sudden increase in fire intensity or rate of spread.

bog race: long-running tradition involving the deepest, sloppiest mudhole around. Veterans pay two dollars to watch as rookies run against each other for the accumulated spoils.

bucket: container that is attached to a helicopter by a cable and used to lift water out of lakes, rivers, pumpkins or retardant pits. They range in size from 400 to 3400-litre capacity and are used to cool flare-ups on the fireline. *See also* pumpkins.

bucking: cutting a tree into sections or to a certain length after it has been felled.

bugging out: *see* evac.

bug juice: insect repellant with watch-melting concentrations of DEET.

buildup: accumulation of fuels on the forest floor (i.e., underbrush, dead trees and duff).

burning off: method of parallel attack. A fireguard is constructed as close to the fire as heat and flames permit. Fuel is then "burned off" between the fireguard and the fire edge.

burn over: when control lines, equipment, structures and sometimes personnel are overcome by the fire.

bush: numbers game played in the bush to determine which sorry loser has to do an unsavoury task.

bush beads: lucky sticks, rocks or carved beads used in the game of bush.

candling: occurs in light timber stands where the

131

bog race

canopy is not continuous and open in stands where the trunks of trees are covered with dead limbs, mosses or lichens, providing a ladder for flames to climb up a tree and quickly consume it.

Cat guard: guard dug by "Cats."

Cats: Caterpillar bulldozers that are used to cut guard by pushing over trees and scoring the ground down to mineral soil. "Cats" are useful in pushing over snags, uprooting burning stumps, rolling over logs and breaking up large piles of smouldering fuel.

chew: chewing tobacco. *See also* monster dip.

Class of '94: high-pitched screech heralding the reunion of members from the elite boot camp of 1994. *See also* old school and lifer.

COC: chain of command. Forest Service infrastructure designed for optimum efficiency and safety (i.e., a crewmember answers to a squad boss who in turn answers to a crew leader who takes direction from a sector or line boss, who ultimately takes direction from the fire boss).

cold trailing: method of determining whether a fire is still burning. It involves careful and methodical inspection of burned material by feeling for heat with your bare hands. Every hotspot must be cold trailed.

conflagration: extreme and aggressive fire behaviour.

control line: any line, including the fireguard, natural firebreaks, retardant lines or all three, from which the fire is being fought.

convection: when a control fire is drawn to the main fire by the principles of convection. The hot air over the fire rises rapidly; cooler air is drawn in to replace it. The inflow of air from the flanks is used to help control the burning of fires.

crack chamois: see tickets.

crew leader: person responsible for the supervision of fire crews on the fireline. *See also* lifer.

crowning: when a fire burns in the upper foliage of standing timber in conjunction with surface fires. In some cases, a running crown fire may develop.

CYA: cover your ass.

direct attack: method used to suppress a slow-moving fire. The fireguard is constructed adjacent to the burning fuel. The fire is attacked and suppressed immediately.

DO: duty officer. A position in the daily rotation in which a crewmember is responsible for answering the fire phone.

drip torch: used to ignite fuel when burning off or back-firing. It drips a flaming mixture of fuel onto forest fuels. Uses a five-to-one diesel and gasoline mixture.

drop siren: warning siren that signals an incoming load of water or retardant dropped by helicopter or air tanker.

dry mop-up: mop-up without the aid of water.

duker: luxurious wilderness outhouse skillfully crafted by a team of wily firefighters.

econo: five-eighth-inch garden hose used in and around the fire. Very mobile and water efficient.

escape routes: preplanned and determined routes to safety away from the fire and its probable path, or the routes back into a previously burned area.

evac: leaving a fire before you are obliged to use your fire shelter.

expanded attack: crews of 20 or more firefighters used on large project fires.

fireline: zone separating burn and non-burn where firefighters work. *See also* control line.

fire shelter: personal tinfoil-like tent designed to protect firefighters from flames and heat for a short period of time. Used only as a last resort, but have saved many lives.

fire triangle: heat, oxygen, fuel. Remove one of these elements and fire cannot exist.

fireweed: not the herb, but the cooking service usually provided on line camps in British Columbia. All B.C. firefighters owe these saints o' the mess a heartfelt thank-you.

FNG: fucking new guy. *See also* rookie.

foam: water expansion agent. Small bubbles of foam hold water to a surface area and lengthen the time it stays there. The foam wraps itself around the burning fuel, adheres to it and subsequently smothers the fire.

foamies: slumber bliss. Thick pieces of foam that reside under your sleeping bag back at fire camp. The thing you think about and dream of all day.

forest fire causes: public recreation, 38 percent; lightning, 37 percent; industrial activity, 25 percent.

Freddies: boil-in-foil meals, grudgingly eaten on the fireline when larger fire camps are not in place.

fuck brush: extremely thick patches of stick alder, devil's club and other nuisance underbrush that tangle and trip you up as you hike steep slopes. It also significantly hampers hand guard construction. Choruses of "fuuuuuuuuck" can be heard from miles around when some unfortunate soul encounters this adversity.

fuel: trees, underbrush and duff.

fuel-break: existing barrier (i.e., road, river, etc.).

Garnet Fire: the fire that occurred in Penticton, B.C., in 1994, in which more than 5,500 hectares were burned, more than 3,500 people evacuated and 18 homes and structures lost. Named in honour of Garnet Grimaldi, a retired firefighter who had worked 38 years with the Ministry of Forests. He passed away at age 61 on July 20, 1994, the same day the fire started.

gourmet guard: hand guard that is easy to dig (i.e., desert, anything that you can scrape or kick down to mineral soil without even using your pulaski). Very rare.

grubbing: using a pulaski to dig up and cool down ashpits, root pads and deep burning duff. A mop-up staple.

gut rot: stomach ache. *See also* chew.

hand guard: fireguard dug by hand (i.e., with pulaskis, shovels or hands).

candling

piss pack

Hansen nozzle: lightweight, compact and versatile nozzle. An industry standard. It has three flow selections and is also handy as an end cap on a hose lay. If a rookie is caught without one they do push-ups.

helipad: temporary structure designed to support the weight of a helicopter. It must have a solid, simple design. Logs are cribbed to create a platform for the machine.

heli-spot: area that is flat and has been cleared for a helicopter to land.

heli-torch: device slung beneath a helicopter that holds jellied fuel in a reservoir and produces burning golf ball-sized particles that are dropped to the ground in order to ignite fuels below.

hello nasty: hollow, burning, flame-throwing tree two-and-a-half metres or more in diameter that you are selected to fall, voluntarily or by bushing. It calls your name. *See also* bush.

hose menders: metal clamps that bind together to stop leaks in charged hose.

hose strangler: device that enables one person to instantly shut off water flow in a charged firehose so the hose can be added to or tapped into. Expert execution will prevent embarrassing wetness.

hose thief: valve that diverts water from the main line of a hose lay to peripheral econo-lines.

Hotshots: United States Forest Service 20-person expanded attack crew. Similar to Canadian Unit Crews.

hotspot: particularly active part of a fire.

hover exit: act of exiting a hovering helicopter by hanging from the skid in order to access terrain where the machine cannot land.

IFR: initial fire report. An assessment completed by the first fire crew on the scene, typically Initial Attack or Rapattack crews.

indirect attack: when the fire crew sets a fire along the inside edge of the control line or natural barrier to consume unburned fuels between the control line and the fire edge (i.e., back-firing).

Initial Attack: three-person attack crews that attend recently ignited spot-fires.

jolly rancher: now defunct term once used to alert firefighters that a fireboss or politician is out on the line. Also known as JRs.

ladder fuels: aerial fuels that quickly ignite, resulting in fast-spreading fires. Serve as kindling to light heavier fuels (i.e., dry branches, needles and brush).

lid: safety helmet.

lifer: jaded vet with a wealth of experience and a penchant for practical joking. *See also* old school.

line camp: camp right on the fireline, where firefighters' tents are set up and where their food is dropped off daily for them to cook.

lined hose: strong, durable hose able to resist tremendous water pressure. Used close to the pump as it is not fire resistant.

line-locate: to flag a path to indicate the direction and path of a fuel-free or Cat guard.

pulaski

machines: helicopters, designated by one of three size categories: light 6, medium 12 and heavy 61.

Martin Mars: legendary, colossal water bombers used as U.S. Naval Air transport planes during the Second World War. Outfitted for forest firefighting after a conglomeration of B.C. forest companies bought them. A Mars bomber skims over water and scoops 27,000 litres into its giant tank. It can drop 270,000 litres of water an hour. Its payload will knock down anything in its path.

melon roll: length of hose rolled in the bush without a stick. Resembles a bruised melon. A rookie move.

monster dip: five-finger pinch of chewing tobacco that fills the mouth. Considered a safety issue by some, or a pleasant experience by the participant.

mop-up: working a dying fire in the final stages. The longest, most monotonous stage, during which firefighters use water, pulaskis, shovels and dirt to fully extinguish a fire.

mozzies: mosquitoes. Satan's messengers. *See also* bug juice.

Nomex: fireproof clothing firefighters wear.

old school: veteran firefighters who maintain crew traditions (good and bad) and pass them on to the new recruits (like it or not). *See also* lifer.

parallel attack: method applied in situations in which a fire is spreading rapidly. Fireguard is constructed as close to the fire as heat and flames permit. Helps to control the fire rather than stop it immediately; serves to reinforce the line.

Parattack: crew that arrives at a fire by jumping out of fixed-wing aircraft. They are equipped with parachutes, protective armour and essential suppression gear. *See also* smoke jumper.

patrol: final scouring of the near-dead fire where crewmembers seek out hidden hotspots using smell, touch, and Global Positioning System-aided infrared scans. *See also* scan.

piss pack: hand-tank pump worn on the back by unlucky recipients. It holds 18 litres and weighs 23 kilograms. Carrying it is a duty one usually receives as a rookie or after losing a bush. *See also* bush.

pre-heat: when a fire festers in a tree's roots. The consequential heat builds until the entire tree literally explodes.

project fire: large fire that two or more Unit Crews attend and that can take as long as a month to control, contain and extinguish.

pulaski: tool invented specifically for forest firefighting. It is a combination axe and grubbing tool. The axe is used for chopping; the grubber, for digging. A firefighter's constant companion and best friend.

pumpkin: large, portable orange water storage container. It holds up to 450 litres of water and resembles an above-ground swimming pool (and, of course, a pumpkin).

ranger tent: large, standard-issue forestry tent that is a common sight at fire camps. It can accommodate up to 20 firefighters in very close quarters.

rank one to six fire ranking:

rank one: smouldering ground fire or creeping surface fire.

rank two: low-vigour surface fire.

rank three: moderately vigorous surface fire.

rank four: highly vigorous surface fire.

rank five: extremely vigorous surface fire or active crown fire.

rank six: blow-up or conflagration; extreme fire behaviour.

Rapattack: three-person crews who rappel out of hovering helicopters to hotspots that are otherwise inaccessible due to terrain and other restrictions.

recci: sizing up a fire. An immediate survey of an area to gain information about all aspects of a forest fire (strategy, safety, etc.).

retardant: nitrogen-based, slippery red-orange substance that, by chemical and physical action, reduces flammability of fuels. Classified as either long or short term. Can turn the forest floor into a skating rink.

RFL: rookie for life.

rookie: eager green clay ready to be moulded. *See also* FNG.

ro-sham-bo: rock, paper, scissors. High-end technology used in task delegation. *See also* bush.

Salmon Arm Fire: one of the worst fires in the history of British Columbia. Occurring in 1998, the blaze damaged more than 6,000 hectares, caused the evacuation of approximately 7,000 people and destroyed 40 buildings.

sawyers: certified firefighters who are responsible for falling and bucking trees during a forest fire.

scan: infrared detection of hot or still-burning pockets within a dying fire. An invaluable tool in patrolling.

shake and bake: see fire shelter.

sippi hole: deepest, sloppiest mud hole around. *See also* bog race.

skidder: vehicle used in the logging industry. It is a highly manoeuverable machine that can operate efficiently and rapidly in very rough terrain. Used primarily as a water carrier for forest firefighting.

smoke jumper: firefighters who access fires via plane and parachute. The smoke jumping program began in the United States and has since been adopted in Canada. *See also* Parattack.

snag: dead or dying tree that is more than three metres in height. Unpredictable and mean.

spot-fire: fire started in advance of the main fire by burning sparks or embers carried from the main fire by wind, convection or by rolling downhill.

squad boss: each Unit Crew is comprised of three or four squads led by the squad boss, who is responsible for their squad's daily objectives, organization and safety.

Stanny: Stanfield wool sweater. An invaluable piece of fireline clothing, practically part of the Forest Service uniform.

tickets

subsurface fire: smouldering fire that burns in duff below ground.

surface fire: fire that burns above ground.

swamping: art of clearing trees and debris that a sawyer has felled to create a fuel-free. A swamper is the person who performs this duty.

SWOB: when the rancid hand of a fellow firefighter finds its way to your unsuspecting nose. Occurs when carrying a heavy load and hands are full.

10:00-a.m. concept: every effort is made to control a wildfire by 10:00 a.m. on the day following discovery. After 10:00 a.m. the temperature increases and we move into the hottest part of the day when the majority of drying and heating occurs.

testing standards:
• **pump-hose test:**
- 100-metre walk with 23-kilogram pump
- 300-metre run carrying four 30-metre sections of one-and-a-half-inch hose
- 200-metre run dragging a fully charged one-and-a-half-inch hose
- finish in under four minutes while wearing boots and Nomex uniform
• **upright rows:**
- 18 repetitions of 23 kilograms, paced with a metronome
• **shuttle run:**
- 20-metre sprints at an increasing speed to a minimum of level 10
• **pack test:**
- replacing the shuttle run. Walk five kilometres in 45 minutes while carrying a 23-kilogram pack

three-way valve: used in a hose lay to split the discharge hose from one line into two separate discharge lines.

Ticker, the: refers to the Garnet Fire of 1994 in Penticton, B.C. *See also* Garnet Fire.

tickets: toilet paper (i.e., "Do you have any tickets for the show?").

Timexed: time when a crew is going to be pulled off a fire for rest days due to fatigue.

Unit Crew: highly trained, mobile, physically fit, highly productive crew of 20 firefighters, able to sustain action for 72 hours before re-supply is needed.

unlined hose: hose made out of a nylon-cotton blend that percolates or weeps so it can be used in the fire area. It is burn-resistant to embers and low-radiated heat.

urban bandit: dust-and-smoke mask that actually works when you get into the nasty stuff. Often too hot to wear unless conditions are extreme.

Wajax Mark 3: industry standard high-volume pump. This pump will run all day if properly primed and fueled. A true workhorse.

Wajax Mark 26: Mark 3's little brother. A lower volume pump, which is effective as a relay pump for the Mark 3.

widowmaker: dead, heavy and hanging tree limb. Can cause serious injury if it falls on the unsuspecting.

FURTHER INFORMATION

FOREST FIRE STATISTICS

Wildfire starts: total number of fires, lightning and human caused:

	BC	YT	AB	NT	SK	MB	ON	QC	NF	NB	NS	PE	PC	Total
1999	1,150	160	1,355	170	735	612	1,002	1,037	228	606	462	34	40	7,591
10 yr avg	2,493	170	911	363	756	554	1,663	928	144	452	391	33	90	8,947

Wildfire hectares: total area burned in hectares:

	BC	YT	AB	NT	SK	MB	ON	QC	NF	NB	NS	PE	PC	Total
1999	10,620	185,956	122,612	550,046	180,820	121,826	328,248	97,747	39,292	1,211	1,822	77	65,368	1,705,645
10 yr avg	34,251	191,443	118,593	967,383	537,796	677,833	253,562	513,326	45,274	1,860	709	101	15,747	3,357,877

Forest fire-related fatalities in Canada:

Year	1986	1987	1988	1989	1990	1991	1992	1993	1994	1995	1996	1997	1998	1999
Fatalities	6	3	3	0	3	4	2	0	2	4	0	0	0	0

Personnel Mobilized in Canada:

Year	86	87	88	89	90	91	92	93	94	95	96	97	98	99
Fire Mgmt	21	12	13	38	14	28	12	10	23	158	156	52	338	241
Overhead	16	8	4	12	8	8	0	0	0	59	68	0	80	49
Specialty	5	4	9	26	6	18	5	10	13	63	60	33	195	164
Liaison	0	0	0	0	0	2	7	0	10	36	28	19	63	28
Sustained Action	84	0	504	141	250	346	230	0	200	647	822	0	847	408
Initial Attack	47	0	100	80	91	85	274	0	200	907	376	390	115	654

Source: Canadian Interagency Forest Fire Centre

Wildfire starts and hectares burned in the United States:

Year	90	91	92	93	94	95	96	97	98	99
Fires	122,043	116,941	103,946	97,030	114,066	130,019	115,166	89,517	81,043	93,702
Hectares	2,207,427	608,095	733,365	934,571	1,913,023	937,475	2,712,089	1,482,076	942,782	2,291,278

Source: National Interagency Fire Center (US)

WEB SITES

Canadian Forest Fire Sites

Canadian Forest Service
www.nrcan.gc.ca/cfs

National Fire Database Program
nfdp.ccfm.org

Canadian Interagency Forest Fire Centre
www.ciffc.ca

The Wildfire Training Network
www.wildfiretrainingnet.com

Canadian Wildland Fire Information System (CWFIS)
fms.nofc.cfs.nrcan.gc.ca/cwfis

Fire Research Network
nofc.cfs.nrcan.gc.ca/fire

Canadian Wildfire Network
www.denendeh.com/flycolor/wildfire

Canadian Forestry Sites

Canada's Forest Network
www.forest.ca

Canadian Institute of Forestry
www.cif-ifc.org/direct.html

Canadian Forests Web Site
www.canadian-forests.com

Northern Forestry Centre of the Canadian Forest Service
www.nofc.forestry.ca

Forest Education B.C. (FORED)
www.foredbc.org

British Columbia Ministry of Forests Protection Branch
www.for.gov.bc.ca/protect

Alberta Environment Forest Protection
www.gov.ab.ca/env/forests/fpd/

Saskatchewan Environment and Resource Management
www.serm.gov.sk.ca/forests/fire

Manitoba Conservation
www.gov.mb.ca/natres/index.html

Ontario Aviation, Flood and Fire Management
www.mnr.gov.on.ca/MNR/affmb/Fire/fire.htm

Quebec Ministry of Natural Resources
www.mrn.gouv.qc.ca/3/35/350/intro.asp

Nova Scotia Department of Natural Resources
www.gov.ns.ca/natr/FORESTRY/forestry.htm

New Brunswick Natural Resources and Energy
www.gov.nb.ca/dnre/

Prince Edward Island Agriculture and Forestry
www2.gov.pe.ca/fire/index.asp

Newfoundland and Labrador Department of Forestry Resources
www.gov.nf.ca/forest/

Northwest Territories Forest Managment
www.gov.nt.ca/RWED/fm/index.htm

Related International Sites

FireNet: The International Fire Information Network
www.anu.edu.au/Forestry/fire/firenet.html

The Fire & EMS Information Network
www.fire-ems.net

Global Fire Monitoring Center (GFMC)
www.ruf.uni-freiburg.de/fireglobe

International Association of Wildland Fire
www.wildfiremagazine.com

National Interagency Fire Center
www.nifc.gov/

PUBLICATIONS

Agee, James K. *Fire Ecology of Pacific Northwest Forests*. Island Press, 1966.

Davies, Gilbert W. and Florice M. Frank. *Memorable Forest Fires: Two Hundred Stories by U.S. Forest Service Retirees*. History Ink Books, 1995.

Fuller, Margaret C. *Forest Fires: An Introduction to Wildland Fire Behavior, Management, Firefighting, & Prevention*. John Wiley & Sons Canada, 1991.

Morrison, Ellen E. *Guardian of the Forest: A History of Smokey Bear & the Cooperative Forest Fire Prevention Program*. Morielle Press, 1996.

Pattison, Lorraine. *The Garnet Fire*. Self-published, 1995.

Pringle, Laurence P. *Fire in the Forest: A Cycle of Growth and Renewal*. Atheneum, 1995.

Pyne, Stephen J. *Introduction to Wildland Fire, 2nd Edition*. John Wiley & Sons Canada, 1996.

Pyne, Stephen J. *World Fire: The Culture of Fire on Earth*. University of Washington Press, 1997.

Pyne, Stephen J. and William Cronon. *Fire in America: A Cultural History of Wildland and Rural Fire*. University of Washington Press, 1997.

Sandberg, David V., John D. Walstad and Steven R. Radosevich. *Natural & Prescribed Fire in Pacific Northwest Forests*. Oregon State University Press, 1990.

Taylor, S.W., et al. *Field Guide to the Canadian Forest Fire Behaviour Prediction (FBP) System*. University of British Columbia Press, 1997.

Teie, William C. *Fire Officer's Handbook on Wildland Firefighting*. Deer Valley Press, 1997.

Theolie, Mike. *The Fireline*. Fulcrum Publishing, 1995.

Wilson, Bill. *Overview and Directory to British Columbia Wildland Forest Fire Protection Industry*. B.C. Ministry of Forests, Research Branch, 1994.

ACKNOWLEDGEMENTS

Throughout the year it has taken to complete this project, we have relied on the help of friends to make it all come together. I'd like to express my heartfelt appreciation for the support of the following individuals — who asked for nothing in return: Isabelle Nanton, who gave me the confidence and direction to get this project started, and for later directing us to Raincoast Books where it came to fruition. Thanks to fellow author and photographer Helen Cyr, who patiently answered the thousands of questions I put to her. I am also indebted to photographer Marvin Nerring, for all the help with scanning, and to Jason Crabb, our good friend, who sacrificed many an evening toiling over a computer and helping us meet our deadlines. I'd also like to express my gratitude to Paul Smithe and all those at the Western Academy of Photography in Victoria, whose encouragement and constructive criticism made me believe in myself. Thanks also to Vogue Studios in Nelson, B.C., for easing the pain of my increasing film demands.

Many thanks to those in the Protection Branch of British Columbia's Ministry of Forests who we interviewed and consulted over the months, especially Jim Mottishaw, Roy Benson, Brad Hartley and Ryan Pascal. Thanks to Jim Dunlop — Director of the Protection Program when this project was in its infancy — who supported this book throughout its growth. Thanks also to Victor Godin of Forest Education BC for believing in this project and for your initial support.

Big thanks to all the firefighters who made this book possible — especially the Valhalla Unit Crew. You struggled through months of having a camera shoved in your faces, invading your lives. Thank you for supporting this project, and for being yourselves and making Valhalla a place none of us will ever forget. Many thanks to my crewleader and friend Mike Allan, who always made special room for my heavy bag of camera gear no matter how tight our weight restrictions, and for bringing me along when something exciting was going down so I could capture it on film. I'd like to thank Alastair Ferries for his fine cuisine and dark humour, despite the demanding, temperamental brats we have all been. Also, I wouldn't be where I am today without my friends and family (especially my parents and brother Chris). You have surrounded me with an atmosphere of positive energy and undying support.

Special thanks to Susan MacPherson for her design talents, her generosity and her limitless patience. While I'm speaking of patience I need to include everyone at Raincoast Books: Brian Scrivener, who initially took us under his wing, and Ruth Linka for her support. Kudos to our editors Derek Fairbridge and Lynn Henry, and to art director Les Smith — thanks for your direction and support. Finally I would like to thank David "The Bastard" Greer, my partner in crime and buffoonery, for his moody, stress-filled antics and for our late-night brainstorming sessions drinking Cinzano, reliving the glory days while enjoying a mid-winter's chew. — Noel Hendrickson

I would like to dedicate my work to my father, Edwin Greer, for his unconditional support, and to my grandfather, John Winton, for inspiring, age-defying energy. I would like to thank all my family and the beautiful and charming Sally Heath. Also, I must thank: Nigel Reeves, #68 Patrick Creelman, Steve "Pipefitter" Dynie, Michael Wrinch, Colin Bates, J. J. Deon, J. J. French, et al. Thanks to Gary Snyder. Thanks to the Beans and the DirtMitts for their musical inspiration and, especially, thanks to all who are Charlie (C. T. and Allan). I would like to thank the Spleen for all of the good times we have had on this project. Finally, thanks to Coastal Unit Crew for introducing me to this gig. — David Greer

ABOUT MY GEAR AND FILM

It never failed — I would always run out of film in the most remote locales and I didn't have much luck finding professional transparency films in places like Dawson City, Yukon, or Chapleau, Ontario. When I ran out I would turn to Kodak Royal Gold 100 ISO as a colour film substitute, which was readily available in most small towns. Primarily I used Fuji Provia and Velvia transparency films, which are relatively grainless and yield highly saturated colours. For black and white print films I used Kodak TCN400 and P3200. The P3200 is one of my favourite films: it has a meaty emotional grain that lends itself to the nostalgic feel present in many of the black and whites.

My primary camera system is the Nikon F-5 with 20mm, 60mm macro and 80 to 200mm lenses, with a rugged Nikonos V and 35mm topside lens as a rainy weather backup. I packed these in a small pelican case that then fit into the daypack that went everywhere with me. The additional gear added an extra seven to 10 kilograms to my load and, through all the cursing and mishaps, I think it was worth the effort. — Noel Hendrickson